Sebastian Kleinschmager

I0019791

Can static type systems speed up programming? An experime
dynamic type systems

Document Nr. V199362

Sebastian Kleinschmager

Can static type systems speed up programming? An experimental evaluation of static and dynamic type systems

GRIN Verlag

1. Auflage 2011
Copyright © 2011 GRIN Verlag GmbH
http://www.grin.com
Druck und Bindung: Books on Demand GmbH, Norderstedt Germany
ISBN 978-3-656-25869-8

University of Duisburg-Essen

Master Thesis

An Empirical Study using Java and Groovy about the Impact of static Type Systems on Developer Performance when using and adapting Software Systems

Submitted to the Faculty of Economics and Business Administration –
University of Duisburg-Essen by

Sebastian Kleinschmager

Submitted on 2011-12-06

Semester: 13 (winter semester 2011/12)

Abstract

Type systems of programming languages are a much discussed topic of software engineering. There are many voices arguing towards static as well as dynamic type systems, although their actual impact on software development is rarely evaluated using rigorous scientific methods. In the context of this work, a controlled experiment with 36 participants was conducted which tried to compare the performance of software developers using a static and a dynamic type system for the same tasks using an undocumented API. The two programming languages used were Java and Groovy. The experiment and its results are analyzed and discussed in this thesis. Its main hypothesis was that a static type system speeds up the time developers need to solve programming tasks in an undocumented API. The main results of the experiment speak strongly in favor of this hypothesis, because the static type system seems to have a significantly positive impact on the development time.

Zusammenfassung (German Abstract)

Typsysteme von Programmiersprachen sind ein vieldiskutiertes Thema in der Softwaretechnik. Es gibt sowohl für statische als auch dynamische Typsysteme große Gruppen von Befürwortern, obwohl der tatsächliche Einfluss beider auf die Softwareentwicklung selten mithilfe strenger wissenschaftlicher Methoden ausgewertet wurde. Im Kontext dieser Arbeit wurde ein kontrolliertes Experiment mit 36 Teilnehmern durchgeführt, um die Performanz von Softwareentwicklern mit einem statischen und einem dynamischen Typsystem anhand gleicher Aufgaben in einer undokumentierten Anwendung zu vergleichen. Die hierfür genutzten Programmiersprachen waren Java und Groovy. Das Experiment und die Ergebnisse werden in dieser Arbeit analysiert und diskutiert. Die Haupthypothese des Experiments besagt dass ein statisches Typsystem die Zeit verkürzt die ein Entwickler benötigt um Programmieraufgaben in einer undokumentierten Umgebung zu lösen. Die Ergebnisse sprechen stark für diese Hypothese, da das statische Typsystem tatsächlich einen signifikanten positiven Einfluss auf die Entwicklungszeit zu haben scheint.

Table of Contents

Table of Contents

Table of Contents

Directory of Figures

Directory of Tables

Directory of Listings

1. Introduction

Software development is generally a complex process that is up to today almost impossible to predict. This is true even if the focus is on the pure programming part of software development and other associated tasks like requirements gathering and specification are ignored. Commonly, software developers need to fix errors or extend an existing program. Both tasks are often summarized as software maintenance and it is stated that software maintenance makes up a significant part of software project costs ([Boehm 1976], [Lientz et al. 1978] and [Gould 1975]). In addition, different programming languages are in use, which in most cases have either a static or a dynamic type system. These two type systems are the source of a controversial discussion in the scientific world as well as in the software industry. Some argue very strongly towards static type systems and the advantages they are supposed to bring, while others oppose these ideas with their own arguments on how these type systems supposedly restrict and complicate the use of programming languages. It is mostly a battle of beliefs, as both sides' arguments are purely speculative and based on logical reasoning. While static type systems have experienced a popularity boost during the last years and are wide spread over many popular programming languages (like Java, C#, C++), there is very little scientific evidence of either their positive or negative impact on software development. This work aims toward closing this knowledge gap a little by conducting a controlled experiment that compares the performance of developers with a static and a dynamic type system on the same tasks. It is not the first experiment conducted on the impact of type systems (others are [Gannon 1977], [Prechelt and Tichy 1998], [Daly et al. 2009], [Hanenberg 2010b] and [Stuchlik and Hanenberg 2011]), but research on the topic is still scarce as the next chapters will show.

The main focus of the experiment is the impact of a static type system on development time, comparing the time needed to solve tasks in Java (which has static type system) and Groovy (using a dynamic type system). For this, several different tasks were designed and all participants of the experiment had to solve all tasks in both programming languages. Three hypotheses were the base of the experiment design. The assumptions were that first, tasks where different classes need to be identified are solved faster in a statically typed language. This was also tested with different numbers of classes to identify. Second, for semantic errors, the kind of type system should not make a difference on the completion time. Third, when using a dynamically typed language, it is assumed that it takes a longer time to fix errors if runtime error occurrence and bug insertion (meaning the location in the code that is faulty and which later results in the runtime error) are farther removed from each other. All this is based on programs that are undocumented, meaning that there are neither comments or documentation, nor variables that explicitly point toward their contained types (more about this notion of no documentation later).

Chapter 2 explains the motivation for this thesis and the general scientific history of empirical research in software engineering (or lack thereof) and also gives some background information on some important topics associated with this work's context. These topics are type systems, maintenance, debugging, as well as documentation in software engineering. The chapter closes with a summary of empirical research and methods with a focus on controlled experiments. Afterwards, chapter 3 summarizes and discusses related work that has previously been conducted on the topic of static and dynamic type systems. In chapter 4, the experiment's research question and design is explained in detail. Afterwards, chapter 5 sums up and discusses some threats to validity of the experiment results. The sixth chapter contains the complete analysis of the gathered experiment data. Then, in the seventh chapter, the experiment results are summarized and discussed. Finally, chapter 8 concludes this work.

2. Motivation & Background

In this chapter, first the motivation for this work is represented, along with some information about certain topics that are directly related to the subject of research. These topics are maintenance and debugging, documentation and APIs, as well as type systems. A summary of empirical research and controlled experiments and the current state of the art in software engineering closes the chapter.

2.1 Motivation

The main motivation of this work is to find out whether static type systems improve developer performance when doing software maintenance. Type systems are said to have some inherent qualities that supposedly support a developer when writing and maintaining code which could lead to faster development. As will be seen later, work on this specific topic is scarce and thus this work was meant to provide more insight on the topic. Also, a part of the motivation is the possible impact of APIs on software maintenance in this context.

2.2 Maintenance and Debugging

2.2.1 Maintenance in a Nutshell

Almost anyone does probably have a very intuitive understanding of what maintenance means. Spoken plainly, to maintain something is to keep it from breaking down or stop doing what it was meant to do. For software maintenance, the IEEE gives a short and understandable definition of the term: *"Modification of a software product after delivery to correct faults, to improve performance or other attributes, or to adapt the product to a modified environment"*, [IEEE 1998]. Not only does it include the purpose of fixing or preventing faults, but also improvements. Interestingly, in a newer version of the standard released together with the ISO, the newly definition states that software maintenance is *"the totality of activities required to provide cost-effective support to a software system [...]"*, [ISO/IEC/IEEE 2006]. A definition that is fuzzy compared to the former, though older one. It is still more appropriate and should serve as the base definition for maintenance in this work. In the newer standard, they also define four corresponding maintenance types: Corrective, Preventive, Adaptive and Perfective Maintenance. Corrective and adaptive maintenance are in the focus of this work.

Something that is related to maintenance but infinitely harder to define is the notion of maintainability. Citing the 2006 standard again (the 98 did not yet define the term), it says that maintainability represents *"the capability of the software product to be modified [...]"*, [ISO/IEC/IEEE 2006]. This definition (along with many similar definitions for maintainability from software engineering literature which will not be mentioned here) is very unclear. Worse, there is still no objective measure for maintainability yet. Many attempts were made to either measure it on a more quantitative base using software metrics (e.g. measuring factors that influence maintainability and infer a measure of maintainability this way) and modeling it on a qualitative base. Both approaches have yet to yield any commonly accepted measure of maintainability [Broy et al. 2006].

Software maintenance is a huge cost factor. Boehm claimed that cost of software maintenance is made up of more than 50% of the total project cost of software projects [Boehm 1976]. There a few more studies that give rough estimates, which range from 40% up to 75% of total project cost (study results summarized by [Lientz et al. 1978]). Although quite a few years have passed, other studies do not give the impression that this has changed. In an older study, Gould cites that about 25% of the time is spent on maintenance/error correction [Gould 1975]. While no current figures could be found that support all these percentages, it can be assumed (and personal experience confirms this) that maintenance still takes up a bulk of a software system's lifetime and cost.

2.2.2 Debugging in a Nutshell

It was made clear that maintenance of software takes up huge amounts of time and money. An important part of the maintenance process is the fixing of errors (corrective maintenance) which are commonly called bugs. Consequently, removing an error from a program is called debugging. There is actually some history on the origin of the term "bug" for an error in a computer program, but it is controversial and shall not play any further role here.[1]

---

[1] Interested individuals might take a look at the article on Wikipedia about the term's origin: http://en.wikipedia.org/wiki/Debugging

There are possible classifications of bugs as well as some research works on debugging approaches and modeling them ([Katz and Anderson 1987], [Vessey 1986] and [Ducassé and Emde 1988] for example). According to them all, the debugging process always involves the following tasks (not necessarily in this exact granularity or order): Reading and understanding program code to locate the possible error source, possibly introduce test outputs, gain enough understanding of the program to find a solution for the problem and test the solution.[1] These tasks become significantly harder when the program to fix was written by someone else or if a long time has passed since someone took a look into the code he has written.

A bug can also be the deviation of a program from its specification, which does not necessarily always lead to an error. So it also important that a programmer knows what the actual intention of the program is to fix this type of bug. Ducasse classifies some of the knowledge that helps in the debugging process, among it the knowledge of the intended program, the knowledge of the actual program, an understanding of the programming language, general programming expertise, knowledge of the application domain, knowledge of bugs and knowledge of debugging methods [Ducassé and Emde 1988].

2.3 Documentation and APIs

2.3.1 Documentation of Software Systems

Before being able to change a program, one must first understand it or at least the part needing change. In other words, gain knowledge about it. Schneidewind says that *"it is a major detective operation to find out how the program works, and each attempt to change it sets off mysterious bugs form the tangled undergrowth of unstructed code"*, [Schneidewind 1987]. So because a good understanding of a program is extremely important for maintenance and debugging tasks, it seems wise to take a look at the documentation aspect of software systems.

---

[1] Quite a few studies have been conducted to research debugging approaches, especially the differences between novice and expert programmers. A good starting point is the work of Murphy et al. Murphy et al. [2008] which also references the most important older studies on the topic.

Understanding a program or relevant parts of it before being able to make changes takes a significant amount of the total software maintenance time, especially if the program was written by someone else. [Standish 1984] claims it to be 50-90% of total maintenance cost, although a more recent study by Tjortjis estimates about 30% of maintenance time was devoted to program comprehension [Tjortjis and Layzell 2001][1]. There are different types of documentation artifacts, like class diagrams, flow charts, data dictionaries, glossaries, requirements documents, and more. But in many cases, the only documentation available is the program code and possibly contained comments.

So, whenever programmers need to change an existing program, *"the automated extraction of design documentation from the source code of a legacy system is often the only reliable description of what the software system is doing"*, [Buss and Henshaw 1992]. This is true not only for the automated extraction. Often programmers have to manually read or at least quickly scan huge parts of the code to understand what is going on. Sousa and Moreira conducted a field study and concluded that among the three biggest problems related to the software maintenance process is the lack of documentation of applications [Sousa 1998], leading to the necessity of reading the code. Similar results concerning the primary usage of code as documentation have been reported by [Singer et al. 1997], [de Souza et al. 2005] and [Das et al. 2007].

It should be mentioned that the decision to use source code as a base for program understanding was not always the first choice, but sometimes rather a last resort due to lack of other documentation artifacts. On the other hand, the study by [de Souza et al. 2005] states that source code was always the most used artifact, no matter if other documentation artifacts existed. This contradicts the notion that code is a last resort documentation. Furthermore, there are many reasons for other types of documentation to be either completely absent or outdated in comparison to the current code base. For example, other artifacts are seldom updated along with maintenance in the code to reflect these changes (even comments or annotations in the code tend to "age"), sometimes due to lack of time, budget or motivation.

---

[1] Buss and Henshaw [1992] cite another paper that claims that „some 30-35% of total life-cycle costs are consumed in trying to understand software after it has been delivered, to make changes". Unfortunately, the original article Hall [1992] could not be retrieved for reviewing.

All these problems are far beyond the scope of this work, which from a documentation view focuses exclusively on the documentation value of the source code. First, source code will always be present even when all other artifacts are missing or outdated, and second it can be assumed that building a cognitive model from code is easier for a programmer. After all, it is what all programmers are used to see regularly. As an interesting side note with practitioner's view on the pros and cons of documenting software, there is a growing community of followers of the so called "Clean Code" initiative. The "Clean Code" approach was originally spawned by Robert C. Martin in his book [Martin 2009]. Basically, he proposes that good source code is meant to document and explain itself, without the need for many comments. Source code should be written in a way that a reader can read it literally like a book, with speaking method and variable names that clearly state their purpose and function.

2.3.2 APIs and Application of their Design Principles in General Programming

Assuming that a programmer only has the available source code as documentation, he needs to make do with what he can get. Depending on the circumstances, there is a difference whether he reuses components from the outside or simply jumps into an existing program and makes changes there. Commonly, if code has been written to be used in different contexts and is in itself a finished component, the part of the code that can be used from the outside is commonly known as the API (Application Programming Interface). An API generally consists of different classes with different methods, along with possible documentation. These need to be public so that they can be used from the outside of the component. Put another way, they are the adapters which should be used to plug the component into another program. The component's internals are usually hidden behind the API classes and methods.

There are many reusable APIs available; Java for example is supplied with its own set of class libraries that provide functionality from printing to a console window to reading and writing files to disk. Most current programs are written with a smaller or larger amount of API usage in them. In this work, programmers did not have to use any specific third-party API, but only the classes given to them, to whom they had full access. This is generally not considered as API usage, although the principles of good API design still apply here. An important rule is given by Henning in [Henning 2007]: *"APIs should be designed from the perspective of the caller"*. He also gives a very important statement which neatly summarizes what APIs are all about: *"Even though we tend to think of APIs as machine interfaces, they are not: they are human-machine interfaces"*, [Henning 2007]. Disregarding for a moment the fact that having complete access to a program's code is not exactly what one would call API use, the same principles should nevertheless apply to all parts of program code in general. It is reasonable to assume that a programmer who has to fix a bug in existing code is often still at a loss when try-ing to understand many functions just by looking at the interface of a class.

2.4 Type Systems

Broken down, the essence of a type system is that it constraints the use of variables and other statements in a program by enforcing them to adhere to a certain type (like con-taining a text, or a number, but not both). Cardelli and Wegner use an interesting meta-phor to describe the fundamental purpose of a type system: *"A type may be viewed as a set of clothes (or a suit of armor) that protects an underlying untyped representation from arbitrary or unintended use."* *[Cardelli and Wegner 1985]*.

Two types of type systems are common, the static and the dynamic type system. The difference between a dynamic and static type system is the time at which the type of an object is actually checked. A programming language implementing a static type system (like Java, C++ or C# to name just a few popular ones) usually has a type checker that can tell the developer if there are any errors in the program based on the static infor-mation in the written code. The code does not need to be executed to find these errors. For example if the programmer tries to put an object of type *Ship* into a variable of type *Car* the compiler can detect this error and tell the programmer. Usually this means a program cannot be run until the compiler can detect no more type errors based on static information. A dynamic type system usually does this check only at runtime. This means the program will run, but as soon as the program tries to tell the *Car* object to *"SetSail"* (a method only a ship would have), the program terminates with a runtime type error.

So the main difference of the two type systems is the time at which a type is checked for its constraints. Sometimes dynamically typed languages are mistaken for untyped/typeless languages, which is wrong. Dynamically typed languages use types, although do not enforce them statically and perform the type check during runtime.

```
Car myCar = new Car();
int number = 5;
string aText = "I am a text";

number = "Number"; //This would result in a compile-time error
```
Listing 2-1: Examples for variable declarations in a statically typed language

```
myCar = new Car();
number = 5;
aText = "I am a text";

number = "Number"; //This is perfectly ok
```
Listing 2-2: Examples for variable declarations in a dynamically typed language

The first of the above code snippets shows some variable declarations and values/objects put into them for a statically typed language. The number variable is declared as type *int*, which means it can store whole numbers. The last line would result in an error during compilation, because the type checker can see that the programmer is trying to put a text into a variable of type *int* and tell him. It thus prevents a possible error during program execution. In the second snippet, the information of what types the variables are of is omitted. It is very possible to put a number into a variable, and immediately afterwards replace its contents with a text. This could lead to a runtime error (if the programmer tries to multiply two variables that contain texts by mistake).

Both systems have their intrinsic advantages and disadvantages, of which some should be discussed here from the viewpoint of static type systems.

Advantages of a static type system (taken from [Cardelli 1997] and [Pierce 2002])

- A static type system prevents the programmer from making mundane type related errors through disciplining him because of the type enforcement. (Cardelli page 6 and Pierce pages 4-5)
- Because of the static type information available they can detect a lot of type related errors (calling a method on a wrong type) during compilation and thus reduce the amount of runtime type errors (Cardelli page 6 and Pierce pages 4-5)

- As another result of the reduced type errors, they also minimize security risks, e.g. by preventing harmful type conversions (Cardelli page 6 and Pierce pages 6-8)

- A static type system can provide the reader of code with an implicit documentation. Because a static type system enforces type declarations for variables, method parameters and return types, it implicitly increases the documentation factor by making the code speak for itself. (Pierce page 5)

- A type system may enable certain forms of optimization by the compiler or the runtime environment because type casts and runtime checks are made obsolete in certain situations. It can thus make the language more efficient (Pierce page 8)

Disadvantages of a static type system (all taken from [Tratt 2009][1] pages 7-10)

- Restrictions on the range of possible applications. Because a type system can be overly restrictive and force the programmer to sometimes work around the type system.

- Limitations on the degree of possible modification during runtime. Statically typed programming languages can only rely on heavily complex reflection operations to be able to be changed during runtime.

- They can get in the way of simple changes or additions to the program which would be easily implemented in a dynamic type system but make it difficult in the static type systems because of dependencies that always have to be type correct.

In addition to the disadvantages taken from Tratt, there is also the general notion of documentation redundancy introduced through the use of static type systems, leading to very verbose code. Simply consider the following example to see the point:

```
StringBuilder stringBuilder = new StringBuiler();
```
Listing 2-3: Redundancy of information through static type system

In the end, both sides have good arguments that are logically coherent. Nonetheless, it remains a conflict of ideologies as long as no reliable results from multiple studies or other scientific methods are available. This experiment focuses mainly on the documentation and error prevention aspect of type systems when trying to shed some light on their advantages and disadvantages.

---

[1] Also see Lamport and Paulson [1999] or Bracha [2004] for more discussions

2.5 Empirical Research in Software Engineering

2.5.1 On Empirical Research

By "research", this work refers to the rigorous scientific research methods that are usually applied in the natural and some of the social sciences and have matured over hundreds of years. Normally, this type of research is driven by the desire of the researcher to answer a question, possibly after observing some condition in reality and then formulating a theory (an explanation) about the nature of this condition. This can include how or why it might have occurred or what it is made of, among other things. Anything occurring in nature or anywhere else can be the subject of such a theory.

Next, a hypothesis is formulated based on the theory which predicts the condition or aspects of it. This hypothesis can be rejected or hardened (it can never be proven) by collecting data relevant for this hypothesis and analyzing it. Do the data confirm the hypothesis, the theory seems more sound, if they contradict the hypothesis, then the hypothesis is considered falsified and has to be rejected (although a new theory based on changed assumptions can be created afterwards). Data collection is commonly done using experiments or other methods of empirical research. Although this approach dates back to Sir Francis Bacon[1] and others that have modified the ideas over time, Karl Popper [Popper 2008], a famous scientific philosopher, is quoted most frequently in this context. Popper believed that experimental observation is the key to scientific discovery and proposed that hypotheses should be falsifiable.

The above described method of scientific research that is concerned with creating theories and hardening or falsifying those using experiments or observations is nowadays commonly called empirical research. The term empiricism is derived from a Greek word for *"based on experience"*. Empirical research uses different methods which also differ between the sciences that apply them, e.g. the natural sciences, psychology, social science and medicine. Each uses different methods and approaches that have proven to produce reliable and valid results in specific areas. The notion of validity means that something really measured what it was made to measure, and reliability means that it

---

[1] His method was published in his book called *"Novum Organum"*. An English translation is available on http://www.constitution.org/bacon/nov_org.htm

measures this something consistently across different conditions (e.g. when taking the measure repeatedly while assuming all other variables are similar, the measured result should be similar for both measures).

2.5.2 Controlled Experiments

Although there are whole books dedicated to the art of creating and designing experiments and studies, only a short summary of controlled experiments is presented here. More information can be taken from [Prechelt 2001], which is a good introduction into experimentation for the software engineering discipline.[1] The following part explains controlled experiments. A summary of more methods can also be found in this authors own Bachelor thesis [Kleinschmager 2009].

The method of research used in this work is a controlled experiment. These experiments try to rigorously control the experiment conditions by keeping as many factors constant as is possibly, while deliberately manipulating only one or a few experiment variables. Conducting a controlled experiment can be very cumbersome and difficult, because planning and implementation take a lot of time and consideration as well as attention to detail.

There are three types of variables in controlled experiments (not to be confused with programming variables): Independent, dependent and the sum of all other variables, sometimes also called *"noise"* or unsystematic variation. The first type, the independent variable, is manipulated by the experimenter and then the impact of the manipulation is measured using the dependent variables (which are called dependent because they depend on the independent variable). Variation resulting from manipulation of the independent variables is called systematic variation. An example would be the time an athlete needs until his heartbeat reaches a certain limit (the dependent variable) depending on what kind of exercise he has to do (the independent variable).

Controlled experiments with humans are especially tricky to design because the human factor introduces an infinite amount of unsystematic variation (for example, the athlete

---

[1] A much more thorough book on research methods and the corresponding evaluation is Bortz and Döring [2006], whose focus is on the social sciences though. Two other books are available that focus on experimentation in software engineering. These are Wohlin [2000] and Juristo and Moreno [2001].

might have slept badly the night before he did the first exercise, but had a very refreshing sleep during the night before the second exercise). Unsystematic variation or *"noise"* can seriously harm the usefulness of any results, and therefore many measures need to be taken in order to reduce them as much as possible. As will be explained later in more detail, one of these measures is to design experiments where all participants partake in all conditions and also in a random or balanced order. This makes it easier to calculate the systematic variation using statistical methods.

All in all, controlled experiments have a high validity and can easily be reproduced many times (when following the exact setup and implementation), producing reliable and comparable results. Their biggest disadvantage is their large cost in time and work for preparation, buildup and evaluation.

2.5.3 Current State of Empirical Research in Software Engineering

Software systems today are getting more and more complex, and more and more expensive to develop. Their impact on everyday life is immense. Cars, planes, medical equipment, computers for financial transactions and almost infinitely more examples of machines or devices depend on software.

Under normal circumstances, one might think that the creation and maintenance of software would be a well-researched and perfected field of work. But in software engineering –sadly-, the situation is quite the contrary. There is a huge deficit of research based on experimenting and hypotheses that can be falsified. In most parts, the current state-of-the-art in the software sciences lacks scientific method, which is insufficient and inadequate for a field that claims to do science. In 1976, Boehm tried the definition of software engineering as: *"The practical application of scientific knowledge in the design and construction of computer programs and the associated documentation required to develop, operate, and maintain them"*, [Boehm 1976]. Intuitively, this definition still fits quite well today, although Boehm leaves open what exactly he means by scientific knowledge. In 1991, Basili and Selby already wrote that the *"immaturity of the field is reflected by the fact that most of its technologies have not yet been analyzed to determine their effects on quality and productivity. Moreover, when these analyses have occurred the resulting guidance is not quantitative but only ethereal."* [Basili and Selby 1991].

In the days of 1991, software engineering was still young and in its early stages and evolution, so it might be alright to say that such a young field had yet to find its scientific base. But, some years later, apparently not much had changed. Lukowicz, et al. did a study on research articles [Lukowicz et al. 1994] and found out that from over 400 articles only a fraction included experimental validation (and there is no mentioning of the quality of the experimental setup and analysis in the other articles). In 1996, Basili again criticized the lack of experimentation and learning, although a few studies had already been conducted. He says that there should be a *"cycle of model building, experimentation and learning. We cannot rely solely on observation followed by logical thought"* [Basili 1996].

The current state is that observation is still mainly followed by logical thought and arguments towards generalization, maybe model building. In some cases, even a field study is conducted, which is commendable, but hardly sufficient for science.

There are many arguments and excuses to not do experiments in software sciences. In 1997, Tichy summarized some of them [Tichy 1997]. Snelting [Snelting 1998] even accuses software scientists of applying constructivism and pleads for a more rigorous methodological research approach in software engineering, but also sees some improvement some years later [Snelting 2001]. So it seems obvious that there is a lot of arguing about which direction the software sciences should go. Both sides do have reasonable arguments (some good examples are [Denning 2005] and [Génova 2010]).

All this does not mean that experiments are the holy grail of science, but the status quo should be that no good model or theory can hold or be generalizable without sound experimental validation. Free speculation and experimentation should work in hand in hand, as is demanded in [Génova 2010], even if he argues strongly towards a more speculative approach. Especially the human factor in software engineering has been neglected for many years, as Hanenberg rightfully criticizes [Hanenberg 2010c]. It is great if people come up with new techniques, models and approaches, as long as they are usable and systematic studies with humans show that it helps them develop better software. Because it is the humans, in this case especially the developers, who have to put all things together and actually implement the software, no matter how great the tool support and theoretical foundation is. The current state of events is that techniques, models and approaches develop (and often vanish) much quicker than they can be validated in scientific experiments.

3. Related Work

This chapter summarizes the results from the few preceding studies available on static type systems. All of the here presented experiments are those that use humans as subjects of the experiment and are specifically targeted on comparing static and dynamic type systems. There are other works which for example focus on using a type checker on a program previously written with a dynamically typed language to check whether these programs contain possible errors [Furr et al. 2009]. Some analyze a large base of open source projects and try to measure programmer productivity based on the language used, like [Delorey et al. 2007]. Others compare the general performance of developers for a task using very different programming languages and/or the runtime performance of the final program [Hudak and Jones 1994], [Gat 2000] and [Prechelt 2000]. But as this work was targeted on evaluating the impact on the performance of developers, only papers that implement a comparable design with humans as participants are mentioned.

3.1 Gannon (1977)

The oldest study that could be found which directly experimented on the impact of type systems was conducted in 1977 by Gannon [Gannon 1977]. It used a simple repeated measures cross-over design with 38 graduate and undergraduate students who had to program the solution to a problem twice; once with a statically typed language and the second time with a dynamically typed language. Both languages were designed specifically for the experiment. The participants were split into two groups, each group starting with a different language and then using the other the second time. The hypothesis was that the reliability of software was enhanced by a language if the errors made by the participants in that language where less numerous than those of the second language. He did not give any clear indication of favoring any of the two languages in the hypothesis.

The methodology used has the advantage of the repeated-measures design by giving the possibility of a within-subject analysis. Although there certainly would have been a carry-over effect because it was the same task that had to be solved both times, so the participants might have already had a "solution roadmap" in their minds after finishing with the first language. His measure against this was to rely on the features of the two languages that were explicitly altered: The dynamically typed language did not include any built-in string functionality, which the participants had to build themselves. It can be argued that this considerably threatens the experiments internal validity because it is not clear if the results measure the impact of the type system or the impact of missing string operations for the dynamically typed language.

Gannon stated that the results were that the statically typed language increased programming reliability and that inexperienced students benefit more from it. They are based primarily on measuring the number of runs in the environment and the number of error occurrences. Only some of the results are statistically significant. In general, the results are questionable, because of the fact that the participants had quite a few problems with the missing string functionality in the dynamically typed language.

3.2 Prechelt and Tichy (1998)

In 1998, Prechelt and Tichy conducted a similar experiment using two different variations of the C programming language [Prechelt and Tichy 1998], one employing static type checking and one employing dynamic type checking. 40 participants (most of them PhD computer science students) were first split into main groups, one working with the type checker, one without. They then employed a slightly more complicated design, where all participants had to solve both parts of the experiment, although each with a different language. Subgroups were assigned which differed in both the order of the tasks (A then B or vice versa) and also the order of the language to use (first with type checker, then without). So in the end, all participants had been split among four roughly equal sized groups.

The tasks were supposed to be short and modestly complex. Their hypotheses were that type checking increases interface use productivity, reduces the number of defects and also reduces the defect lifetime. They made sure that the programmers were familiar with the language, so that the majority of problems would result from using the rather complex library they were given to solve the tasks. Dependent variables were the number of defects that were introduced, changed or removed with each program version and put them into different defect categories. In addition, the number of compilation cycles and time till delivery were measured.

The results strengthened all their hypotheses and they concluded that type checking increases productivity, reduces defects and also the time they stay in the program. This is based primarily on the number of defects in the delivered programs as well as the reduced defect lifetime that was achieved through the static type system. While the results seem sound from a methodical point of view, there are possible sources of strong unsystematic variation. They discuss some of them, including the learning effect they definitely measured. But (without having the exact task implementations to look at) it seems that -judging from their rough description of the two tasks- that the difference between them could have been a strong source of unsystematic variation. This is a fact they did not mention. Nevertheless, it is still one of the few methodologically sound experiments conducted on type systems and deserves approval, especially because it was the second experiment on the topic ever.

3.3 Daly, Sazawal and Foster (2009)

Many years later, in 2009, Daly, Sazawal and Foster [Daly et al. 2009] conducted a small study using the scripting language Ruby, which is dynamically typed, and Diamond Ruby, a static type system for Ruby. They had four participants and their design was also a repeated-measures cross-over design. All participants were said to be familiar with Ruby and were recruited from a user group of practitioners. In contrast to the other studies mentioned here, they only ran a qualitative analysis on the results without any statistical measures (which would not have yielded any useful results with only four participants anyway).

They could not find any specific advantage of the type system. Apart from some threats to validity that the authors' already mentioned themselves, there again is the difference between the tasks that might have introduced some random effect, even if the authors claim that they were of approximately similar complexity (one was a simplified Sudoku solver and one a maze solver). What is more, the first participant was not given starter code and therefore only solved a fraction of the total tasks' work. And he also did not have internet access, which the experimenters realized was a mistake and made it accessible for the next three; both very possible sources of unwanted effects.

Although the results of the study are more or less exploratory and only qualitative, the authors could induce an interesting hypothesis from their analysis: They reason that in small scale applications like the one from the experiment developers can compensate for the lack of a type system by relying on their own memory or by giving meaningful names to variables and other code artifacts. This is an interesting hypothesis which would be worth testing in a larger experiment.

3.4 Hanenberg (2010)

Another huge experiment was conducted in 2009 by Hanenberg [Hanenberg 2010b], [Hanenberg 2010a]. In his experiment, a total of 49 participants (undergraduate students) had to solve two tasks of writing a scanner and a parser in a language called Purity specifically written for the experiment in a statically and a dynamically typed version. The hypothesis was that the statically typed language would have a positive impact on the development time. He used an independent (between-subject) design where every participant only solved the two tasks once with either the statically or the dynamically typed language. The reasoning behind this design was that participants would probably be biased toward the same language with a different type system after having used it with another type system already.

Compared to the other previously mentioned experiments, where the total experiment time was about four hours per participant, here they had 27 hours of working time (about 45 hours when including teaching time). He also took a different approach by making the time a fixed factor, because the 27 hours were the maximum time given to the participants, in contrast to other experiments were participants usually had as many time as needed. It was also designed in a way that it was very hard to actually fulfill all requirements in the provided time frame.

The results were that the type systems never had a significantly positive impact on the result, in once case of the tests even produced a significantly negative impact, even though this did not lead to overall significantly negative results for the type system. Concerning threats to validity, Hanenberg discusses quite a few of them in detail. But it should be noted that a huge threat to the validity of the results that Hanenberg already mentioned himself is the amount of unsystematic variation that possibly lurks in the independent design of the experiment. Because no within-subject comparison is possible, any differences between the two type systems' performance could also have been due to differences in participant quality and many other factors which could have interfered with measuring the intended effect.

3.5 Steinberg, Mayer, Stuchlik and Hanenberg - A running Experiment series

Next, it should be mentioned that a set of experiments was conducted at this institute and they form an experiment series that focuses on the comparison of static and dynamic type systems. Some of them are mentioned with their description and some preliminary results in a summarizing report [Hanenberg 2011]. This thesis can be considered a part of the series, too.

3.5.1 Steinberg (2011)

One of the still unpublished experiments (the Master thesis by Steinberg [Steinberg 2011]) investigated the impact of the type system on debugging for type errors and semantic errors with 30 participants in a repeated-measures cross-over design. It turned out that the type system speeded up the fixing of type errors, and no significant difference was discovered for fixing semantic errors. This could be considered a success, although some contradicting results were achieved that falsified one of the hypotheses which stated that the farther the code that is responsible for the error is away from the point where the error actually occurs, the greater the fixing time should be. The study might have suffered from a huge learning effect and other factors like a larger influence of the kinds of programming tasks on the unsystematic variation.

3.5.2 Mayer (2011)

The second still unpublished experiment (the Bachelor thesis by Mayer [Mayer 2011]) has the hypothesis that a static type system aids in the use of an undocumented API and shortens the time needed for a task. Again, a two group repeated measures design was used and 27 participants took part. The results were at the time of this work's writing not finished, but initial results revealed rejection of the hypothesis for some tasks and confirmation for others. Again, the results seem inconclusive for the experiment.

3.5.3 Stuchlik and Hanenberg (2011)

Despite the fact that some work is still underway and unpublished, one of the earlier experiments of the series already spawned a separate publication [Stuchlik and Hanenberg 2011] and therefore deserves a deeper look: In the experiment, 21 participants (undergraduates) had to solve 7 Tasks in random order in Java as well as in Groovy. For each language, an own application was used to reduce the learning effect that decreased usefulness of the results in further experiments, even if the two application where structurally equal, only the methods and classes were renamed. One of the assumption was that the more type casts would be needed for a task with a static type system, the larger the difference would be in time taken between the static and the dynamic type system.

Two of the tasks had to be discarded for the analysis because of many comprehension problems with the task descriptions, resulting in a lot of variation. But the results show that there was a significant positive impact of the dynamic type system for some of the tasks. Their reasoning is that type casts are not a trivial aspect of static type systems and need some intellectual effort on part of the developer (even though the results of the better Java developers in the study did not show this effect). Additionally, the initial assumption that more type casts also lead to longer development time had to be rejected, leading the authors to reason that for larger tasks type casts do not play such a major role as they were assumed to.

One of the study's problems was that the tasks were rather constructed tasks that forced the use of type casts were some developers would argue they would not have been needed in a real application. The combined analysis of both groups as one set is also rather problematic, but this fact was already mentioned by the authors and only makes up a small part of the analysis. Using the development time as the major dependent variable is also problematic from the view that software development is usually so much more than just trying to solve a programming task as quickly as possible, but that fact can be overlooked because it was designed as a controlled experiment where as many factors as possible need to be fixed. Also, there are no other objective measures that can be applied to software.

4. The Experiment

Chapter 4 gives an overview of the complete experiment structure along with the specific research question(s) behind its design. The mentioned research question and the hypotheses are explained first, followed by the experiment overview. The overview starts with a short argumentation and some thoughts on the reasons for this experiment design. It also includes some considerations on the use of students as subjects. It then explains the design starting with the questionnaire, the hard- and software environment and last the involved application and exact task categories and descriptions. A short summary of the experiment implementation concludes the chapter.

4.1 The Research Question

In experimenting, a certain question drives the researcher to formulate one or more hypotheses he then strives to test. As already stated, this work is concerned with questions regarding different developer performance with static and dynamic type systems of programming languages. There have been other experiments aiming in the same direction at this institute, which this work builds upon and tries to deepen the insight on the matter. These mentioned experiments are described in [Steinberg 2011] and [Mayer 2011] (or a summary [Hanenberg 2011]) and have already been explained in more detail in the related work part. The first work was actually the one that led to the creation of the development and measurement environment that was used in the second one and in this experiment. The following hypotheses are similar to some hypotheses from these earlier works.

One assumption behind the first hypothesis is that a static type system documents code and makes programming tasks easier. The way the "make easier" part was measured in this experiment was through the development time it takes a participant to solve a programming task. This leads to the first hypothesis:

Hypothesis 1:

Participants solve a programming task with an undocumented API faster when using a statically typed language.

Hypothesis 1 was used in both preceding experiments and could be verified in the second (by Mayer). A similar conclusion could be made in the first, although only targeted at tasks involving debugging, which is the reason why this experiment reused the hypothesis: In the hopes of gaining more insight and hopefully verify the results from the second experiment.

The second assumption is that a type system makes debugging an application easier, but only in certain cases. In other cases, it can be assumed that a static type system does not give any significant advantage for debugging. This leads to two hypotheses and separate measurements.

Hypothesis 2-1:

The further away an actual error is from the bug that is its source, the longer it takes for a participant to fix it when using a dynamically typed language.

Hypothesis 2-2:

It takes the same time to find and fix a semantic programming error no matter whether the language used is statically or dynamically typed..

Hypothesis 2-1 is specifically targeted at dynamically typed languages, as that kind of error it describes leads to a compile-time error in statically typed languages. So the notion of "distance" between a bug and it resulting in an error does not apply in a static type system. A similar hypothesis could only be partially verified in Steinberg's experiment.

Hypotheses 2-2 however, aims in the other direction, by assuming that for semantic errors, it should make no difference whether the error is searched in a statically or dynamically typed language. Having type information should not significantly aid in finding these errors. This was also verified in the first experiment by Steinberg.

4.2 Experiment Overview

4.2.1 Initial Considerations

One thing that needs mentioning about experiment design is the fact that some experiments in computer science use a problematic design (one example can be found in [Wohlin 2000] and some more are summarized in [Juristo and Moreno 2001]). In experiments, the goal is to test an assumption or theory by measuring a certain effect when changing one factor of the experiment and keeping everything else constant (so as to not have any other side effects on the results).

To demonstrate the problem of unwanted side effects, the following fictive design for an experiment similar to this one should be considered: The participants are split into two groups, one group that solves only the Java tasks and one Group that solves only the Groovy tasks. In this experiment, the -simplified- goal is to measure developer performance depending on the language used. The used language is the independent variable which is manipulated by the experiment designer. The importance here lies on the fact that each group only completes either the Java or the Groovy part, not both. The problem with such a design (called independent design or independent-measures design) is that without being able to compare a participants' performance in both parts, it cannot be said whether the results of two participants from separate groups are different because of the programming language they used (systematic variation) or if one was simply a really good programmer or had a lucky day, the other was a bad programmer or had a bad day or any other random factor (unsystematic variation). To demonstrate this difference, the appendix contains an analysis of this experiment by treating the results as if it had used the independent-measures-design just described (A.3).

It should be mentioned that some of these experiments very probably ended up with a threatened validity because no one or at least very few people in the software engineering area actually have any experience in designing and analyzing experiments. By criticizing these designs, not the effort of conducting an experiment is criticized (an effort which is commendable and should be given credit, considering the circumstances), but the validity of some of the results. Implementing an experiment is a hard piece of work and all experimenters in software engineering are still in the middle of a learning process. This work is no exception to the rule. Even if it may benefit from mistakes others made, it itself might someday be found faulty in some part. This can never be ruled out and the ultimate goal for all experimenting researchers should be a sound experimental methodology for software engineering.

However, to finally argue towards the actual design of this work's experiment, there is a method to cope with the problem of unsystematic variation called repeated-measures designs. In these kinds of designs, participant performance is measured with all values of the independent variable (some say under all treatments/conditions). This means participants need to complete all tasks with both languages. Also, participants are commonly to the groups randomly. Now there are two effects at work in the results, one is the manipulation of the independent variable between both parts and one summarizes all kinds of other effects that might influence the second part the participant completes. In general, the manipulation effect should be much stronger. Hence, this kind of design was used in the experiment.

4.2.2 Further Considerations: Studies on Using Students as Subjects

Related work that does not directly correlate with what is done in this study but may have an important impact on its validity is research on using students as subjects in programming experiments. Many studies in software engineering do use students as experiment subjects/participants and this work is no exception. This raises some questions about the possible impact of using students in these experiments and how this might influence how their results can be interpreted as well as their validity. A general discussion about the problem can be found in [Carver et al. 2003] and some of the studies are summarized here, although only those with an explicit focus on programming/software development.

In 2003, a first study was conducted by Höst, Regnell and Wohlin [Höst et al. 2000]. Students and professional software developers had to solve non-trivial tasks where they had to assess the effect of different factors on software development project lead-time. They only found minor differences in the conception and no significant differences in correctness between the two groups.

Also in 2003, Runeson [Runeson 2003] did a study comparing the results of freshmen and graduate students and relating them to results from an industry study. It involved solving a set of programming tasks with growing complexity and two main hypotheses focusing on improvement during the task levels and on the general performance. Their results were that improvements between the task levels was similar for all three groups (freshmen, graduate, industry) but that the freshmen students need significantly more time to fulfill the tasks than graduates students (no comparison was done with the industry group).

Staron did some research in 2007 trying to evaluate whether the students that are used as subjects in software engineering experiments improve their learning process by participating [Staron 2007]. He used a survey to find out the subjective impact that the students felt the experiment had on them and whether they benefitted from partaking. The results show that students generally perceive the experiments as positive and very useful und that their learning benefitted from it.

It can be concluded that students are valid subject in experiments, especially when considering one important point. What is important is the within-subject data of the experiment, not necessarily the between-subject comparison. This means that even if students solve tasks slower than professionals, it makes sense that they do so consistently, meaning both parts will be solved slower by a student. But this should not have any impact on the within-subject analysis.

4.2.3 Design of the Experiment

After deciding on the design of the overall experiment (the repeated-measures approach, as explained above), the tasks were distributed according to the design. All in all, 9 Tasks were part of the controlled experiment. These tasks had to be repeated in both languages, so that nine tasks formed one part in one programming language, the other nine were the corresponding group for a different programming language. This also means the main independent variable was the programming language, its two values being Groovy and Java (representative for dynamic and static type systems). Again, the experiment's dependent and independent variables should not be confused with the programming variables in the programs. Although the tasks were similar for both languages, the complete program was modified by renaming all code artifacts for the second language to obfuscate this. In addition, to make the application completely undocumented, variable names were modified so that they did not match the types they contained (more on this approach during the task descriptions). The variable names in the programs were still chosen to represent a useful domain aspect, but did not point to their exact contained types. The dependent experiment variable that was used to measure the performance was the time the participants needed for the tasks. In addition to the regular tasks, a small warm-up task was provided for each programming language, so that the participants could familiarize themselves with the experiment environment as well as the task descriptions and the programming language.

The tasks were numbered from 1 to 9 (the Java part) and 10 to 18 (the Groovy part). This numbering system was used primarily to give participants the impression that they are really working on different tasks, not the same in both languages. Every participant had to solve both experiment parts and fill out a questionnaire in order to have completed the experiment (more information on the questionnaire results and the participant demography in the appendix under A.2.6). The order in which the participants had to fulfill the tasks was based on the two parts chosen in a randomly alternating order, so that one group of all participants started with the tasks in Java, and another with the Groovy tasks. Inside the experiment parts, the tasks had to be solved strictly in ascending order: A participant starting with Groovy therefore solved first tasks 10 through 18, and then 1 through 9. The blocking can be summarized in a simple table:

Group	Task Order (T1-9 = Java, T10-18 = Groovy)
Group1 (GroovyStarters)	10, 11, 12, 13, 14, 15, 16, 17, 18, 1, 2, 3, 4, 5, 6, 7, 8, 9
Group2 (JavaStarters)	1, 2, 3, 4, 5, 6, 7, 8, 9, 10, 11, 12, 13, 14, 15, 16, 17, 18

Table 4-1: Experiment Blocking Design

It is important to note than in most of this work the tasks will be referred to by the numbers 1 through 9, not 1 through 18, as the latter numbering was only introduced to obfuscate the similarities of the two parts.

A learning effect was anticipated in the design; even if measures were taken to minimize it (like renaming everything in the application, but more about the environment and the task design later). Nevertheless, the nature of the similar tasks in both languages was bound to produce some kind of learning effect. That is why this kind of within-subject design was chosen: To have two groups to compare and detect the learning effect. The impact of this learning effect and its interaction with the experiment design is depicted in Figure 4-1, which was taken from the mentioned related work by Stuchlik and Hanenberg.

It should be a reasonable assumption that the Java starters group would benefit from a learning effect when solving the Groovy part (keeping in mind that a definite learning effect was to be expected). But the additional effort needed to solve the tasks with Groovy (remembering hypothesis 1) should either cancel out that learning effect (resulting in approximately similar times for both Java and Groovy) or be weaker (so that the Java starter would still be slightly slower with Groovy after Java). For the group starting with Groovy however, they should benefit from the learning effect and the positive effect of the type system when solving the Java (their second) part. So here the two effects should add up and result in definite favor of the static type system language Java.

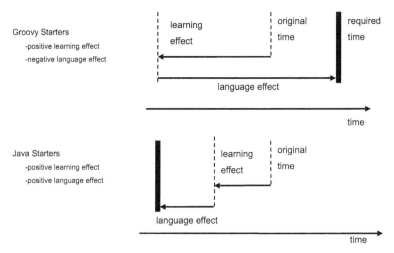

Figure 4-1: Assumed occurrence of learning effect in experiment design (Figure taken from [Stuchlik and Hanenberg 2011])

The participants were given specific instructions during their introduction to the experiment, which included explaining the environment and editor, as well as possible does and don'ts in the experiment context. E.g. they did not need to write their own classes, just modify or use existing ones, no native API classes had to be used. They also received a picture of the two applications with some annotations to explain the underlying domain model.

4.3 Questionnaire

The questionnaire that was handed out to all participants consisted of two parts: The first was the Big Five questionnaire, also called the NEO-FFI [Costa 1992] and the second part was made of a few questions about the participant's programming experience. The Big Five questionnaire was chosen because it is one of the most popular and widely used psychological tests. It tries to measures five personality dimensions called "Openness to Experience", "Conscientiousness", "Extraversion", "Agreeableness" and "Neuroticism", each with its own set of questions that altogether sum up to about 60 questions.

Evaluation of the questionnaire data was not planned to be part of the experiment but it made a lot of sense to gather as much additional data as possible for future research and analysis. The NEO-FFI part was included for a possible exploratory analysis of personality traits/types and experiment performance, and the programming experience part was mainly included to serve as additional data for possible grouping and a meta-analysis of participant questionnaires from different experiments. The latter is a continuation of work already done by this author and Hanenberg [Kleinschmager and Hanenberg 2011], where participant questionnaire data was correlated to participants' performance in the experiments to try to find meaningful connections.

4.4 Hard- and Software Environment

4.4.1 Environment

All participants completed the study on the same Lenovo R60 Thinkpad Computers which were provided by the University, along with a mouse for every laptop.

The prepared software environment was installed on an 8 GB USB Stick. It was a Ubuntu Live Installation of Version 11.04, configured and intended to run and boot only from the stick. The only applications/libraries that were installed apart from the experiment application were XVidCapture (a tool used to record screencasts of the whole experiment for each participant) and the Sun Java Runtime and SDK of Version 1.6_25. The videos from the screen logging application were used as backup for potential problems during the experiment and as a source of information that could give answers to questions which an analysis of the log files alone could not provide.

The experiment IDE (integrated development environment) itself was called Emperior, an editor specifically designed for empirical programming experiments (it was originally created by Steinberg for his master thesis [Steinberg 2011], where it is also explained in much more detail). Emperior provides very simple editing features like a search function or syntax highlighting and also logs different types of information into log files which can be analyzed later.

When the participants clicked on either the "Test" or the "Run" buttons, Unix bash (command-line) and Ant (a Java library for batch and command-line processing, [Apache Foundation]) scripts worked behind the scenes. Both were tasked with setting correct paths variables, compile the application, test projects and return possible run output to the console or call JUnit (a unit testing library for Java, see [JUnit]) to show the test results.

4.4.2 Programming Languages

The two programming languages used were Java and Groovy, whereas Groovy was only used as a "dynamically typed"-Java, meaning that no functions and language features specific to Groovy were used except the dynamic type system. A short summary about both languages is provided here.

4.4.2.1 Java

The third edition of the Java language specification states that *"The Java Programming language is a general-purpose concurrent class-based object-oriented language..."* [Jones and Kenward 1989]. In [Gosling and McGilton 1996], the design goals of the Java environment are summarized roughly to make Java "simple, object-oriented, and familiar", "robust and secure", "architecture neutral and portable", "high performance", "interpreted, threaded and dynamic". It is statically typed and includes automatic memory management by use of a garbage collector and compiles to an intermediary language commonly called "byte code", which is then run by the Java Virtual Machine. It can run on different operating systems, is generally considered easy to learn and there are no licensing or other costs connected with using it.

```
public void helloWorld() {
    String name = "Peter";
    System.out.println(name);
}
```

Listing 4-1: Simple Java Code Example

4.4.2.2 Groovy

Groovy first appeared in 2003 as a dynamically typed scripting language which is based on the Java platform [Strachan 2003] and is since then still under development by an active community (see [Codehaus]). The fact that it is based on Java made it the ideal candidate for the experiment, as it would save a lot of work not having to use completely separate environments, syntax and framework for both parts.

Listing 4-2 demonstrates the dynamic nature of Groovy: The *def*-keyword is used as a dynamically typed variable which can be assigned an instance of any type at any given time no matter what type has been assigned earlier. In addition, in the case of no return type, *void* can be omitted. Method parameters do not need to typed, either.

```
public helloWorld() {
    def name = "Peter";
    System.out.println(name);
}
```

Listing 4-2: Simple Groovy Code Example

4.5 Workspace Applications and Tasks

As already stated in the overview, a total of 18 tasks had to be completed by the participants, nine of which needed to be solved in Java (designated 1 through 9) and nine in Groovy (designated 10 through 18). It was chosen in a simple alternating manner whether a participant started with the Groovy or the Java tasks. The applications that the participants had to work on will be called workspace applications.

4.5.1 The Java Application - A Labyrinth Game

The original program that was used as a base for the participants to use as API and to complete their tasks on was a small round-based video game written in Java for this author's bachelor thesis [Kleinschmager 2009]. Figure 4-2 shows the game window along with some annotations that were given to the participants. In this video game, the player controls a character and has to move through a labyrinth that is riddled with traps and has to get from a start to a goal for each level. Most of the actual game concepts like gaining experience or fighting monsters were not or at least not fully implemented, although enough was finished to give the impression of a real working application.

The video game was then taken apart and customized for the needs of the experiment. Among these changes was the removal/addition of specific classes or methods from the task workspace as well as a complete rework of certain areas of the application. This was to ensure that participants did not accidentally see or use parts of the application that would be required in later tasks. Thus, for each task, certain new methods or classes were added to the workspace application. This heavily modified labyrinth game was the workspace application for the Java part of the experiment.

Figure 4-2: The labyrinth game interface along with some annotations for the participants

4.5.2 The Groovy Application - A simple Mail Viewer

After all tasks had been created for the Java application, the second application of the experiment had to be designed in Groovy. This was achieved by taking the now modified first application and renaming all its classes and methods and other code artifacts so that it would turn into an application with a completely different domain model. In this case, it was reformed into a simple e-mail viewer. This approach ensured that for both the Java and Groovy tasks, what ultimately was edited by the participants consisted of an almost identical structure. The concepts of the game were therefore mapped to concepts contained in a mail viewer. E.g. what was a player in the game moving on a game board was now a cursor on the mail document moving along different tags and content.

Additionally, all type information for variables, return types and method parameters was removed from the application to give the impression of an application written in a dynamically typed language. All error messages were rewritten, task descriptions and explanations modified, so that they would not contain the same wording used in the Java application.

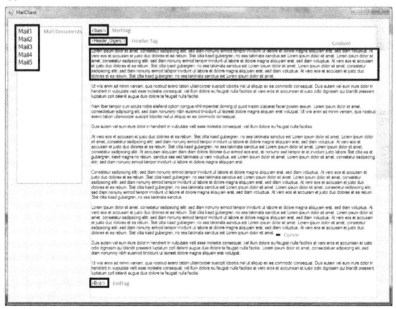

Figure 4-3: The mail viewer interface along with some annotations for the participants

4.5.3 Important Changes made to both Parts

Some additional restructuring and obfuscation was done to both applications to minimize the danger of participants easily noticing that both the Java and Groovy applications were actually almost the same code just with different names. As was already mentioned above, the variable and method parameter names for both applications were also modified so that variable names did not specifically point to the types they contained. Most of the time synonyms and paraphrasing were used for the variable names to make the APIs really undocumented (removing documentation value of variable names, at least concerning their supposed type). E.g a variable that was to contain an instance of the type *LevelType* was named *"levelKind"* so that it did not specifically point the reader to the required class, but still represented a reasonable naming choice in the application domain. One could argue that this kind of renaming might lead to additional noise in the final results, and an even stricter approach would be necessary (like giving them completely useless names like "a", "b", "x"). But the assumption was that the scenario should provide a degree of realism that could very probably also be encountered in a real application, where variable names do not point to their types, but a domain artifact.

4.5.4 The Tasks

4.5.4.1 The Task Types

Next is an overview of the task types and the additional variables. There are three task classes into which the tasks are categorized which need to be explained. These categories are *type identification, semantic errors* and *latent type errors,* they were designed for the different hypotheses and two of them also introduce an additional independent variable because of this. Each task is explained in more detail later, but the task categories and their relation to the hypotheses are described here.

Type Identification

During tasks of the category *type identification* the participants had to identify and create a number of class instances of different types and had to put these together in a single instance or multiple instances. E.g. create a new instance of a class that needed two other types via its constructor.

The new independent variable introduced for this task category was the number of types that had to be identified. Tasks 1, 2, 3, 6, 8, (Java) and 10, 11, 12, 15, 17 (Groovy) belong into this category, making up the majority of the tasks. With rising task number, more types had to be identified, ranging from 2 up to 12 types to be found. For all these tasks, the solution had to be put into the provided method of the Task class in the task package.

Tasks of this type were included for hypothesis 1 (the static type system speeds up development time), although their growing number of types to identify was included to provide more granular data to compare between static and dynamic type systems in case results were mixed.

Semantic Errors

Semantic error tasks contain a semantic error in the application that leads to wrong or unexpected behavior. Semantic errors (sometimes also called logic errors) do not lead to compile-time errors like syntactic errors do. An example could be accessing an array index larger than the total array size or while in the wider sense of semantic errors used in this work an example could be also the missing call to a remove method, leading to duplicate references to one object in the program.

Tasks of this type are included for hypothesis 2-2 (no difference for semantic errors between static and dynamic type system), although there was no additional quantifiable variable introduced for these tasks. As a positive side effect, they might have reduced a general learning effect by providing different kinds of tasks to the participants. The tasks 4, 5 (Java) and 13, 14 (Groovy) belong into this category.

Latent Type Errors

In the case of these errors, latent means that there is an explicit distance between the cause of an error and it resulting in a program failure or defect. These errors were designed so that an instance of a type was being passed to a method that accepted a very different type. This design leads to a compile time error for a statically typed language like Java, which should generally be very easy to find. But in a dynamically typed language like Groovy, this wrong type leads to a runtime error as soon as some other part of the code tries to call a method on this wrong type which it does not possess, making it a very hard problem to find in the Groovy part. This category contains tasks 7, 9 (Java) and 16, 18 (Groovy). The additionally introduced independent variable here was branch size. Tasks of this type were designed for hypothesis 2-1 (which states that a greater distance between bug insertion and runtime error lead to a longer fixing time in a dynamically typed language).

The branch size variable needs some explanation. It was introduced and explained in [Steinberg 2011] and is closely coupled to the stack size variable. The stack size variable is the distance between the location where the bug was inserted and the place on the call stack where it leads to an error in the program. The following code was inspired by Steinberg's example.

```java
public methodA() {
    return 66; //bug insertion
}

public void methodB(param) {
    methodC(param);
}

public void methodC(param) {
    if (param.contains("String")) //place where error occurs
        System.out.println("true");
    else
        System.out.println("false");
}

public void main() {
    def result = methodA();
    methodB("String"); //valid method call resulting in output
    methodB(result); //method call resulting in error
}
```

Listing 4-3: Example code to explain stack and branch size

Considering the given code in Listing 4-3: The *main* method first calls *methodA*. Now, *methodA* is on the stack and returns immediately (with the bug, a number that is returned instead of a String). At this moment, the stack size was 1 (or 2, if the main method counts, but in this experiment the source method is not counted), the method only method on the stack was *methodA*. The second call to *methodB* does not result in any error. So in the final line of *main*, *methodB* is called with the invalid parameter and then calls *methodC*, leading to a runtime error in *methodC* because the integer value in the result variable does not have a method *contain*. At this point, the stack size is 2 again (*methodB* and *methodC*). Now, essentially, the branch size for this error is the size the stack had during bug insertion (only *methodA* was on the stack during bug insertion, thus branch size is 1). So, to summarize, the example has a stack size of 2 and branch size of 1 for the included error. The following figure also depicts the whole sequence.

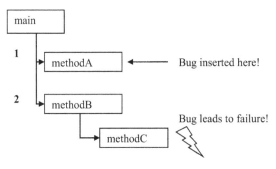

Figure 4-4: Simplified call stack containing bug creation and runtime error

The next part is the explanation and description of all tasks in detail. As every Java task had a corresponding Groovy task which essentially had the same content, the tasks will be explained in their respective pairings. For all tasks a task package with a Task class was provided, which contained the task description as a comment.

4.5.4.2 Tasks 1 and 10 – 2 Types to identify

The first tasks of both parts were relatively simple tasks. 2 types had to be identified. A class of instance *GameManager* (Java) or *MailEditorServer* (Groovy) was passed to the method in the *Task* class, and it had be initialized with a dependency to another class *ActionsAndLoggerPipe*, which itself had to be constructed with two instances of a *Pipeline* class, one with a generic parameter of type *String*, one with a generic parameter of type *Job*. The following Listing 4-4 shows the solution for the Java part (Task 1).

```
public void initializeServer(MailEditorServer server) {
    Pipeline<String> stringPipe = new Pipeline<String>();
    Pipeline<Job> jobPipe = new Pipeline<Job>();

    ActionsAndLoggerPipe actionsLoggerPipe =
        new ActionsAndLoggerPipe(stringPipe, jobPipe);
    server.setActionsAndLogger(actionsLoggerPipe);
}
```

Listing 4-4: Solution to task 1 (Java)

The difference in Groovy (except for the different class names) was that no generic type parameters were needed, so just two different instances of the *GameQueue* (the Groovy countpart of the *Pipeline*) had to be used. So in Groovy it was not clear which type was contained in the manager instance passed to the method, meaning that the participants also had to find the correct class.

```
public def configureManager(def manager) {
    def messages = new GameQueue();
    def commands = new GameQueue();

    def tasksAndMessages =
        new TaskAndMessageQueue(messages, commands);
    manager.setTasksAndMessages(tasksAndMessages);
}
```

Listing 4-5: Solution to task 10 (Groovy)

4.5.4.3 Tasks 2 and 11 – 4 Types to identify

Tasks 2 and 11 raised the number of types the participants had to identify to 4. In the Java part, participants had to put a start and end tag to an instance of type *EMailDocument* and also outfit it with an encoding. The *MailStartTag* and *MailEndTag* classes had to be initialized with a position using the *ursorBlockPosition* class. The encoding part of the task was not explicitly mentioned in its description, but was demanded by the test case, so participants had to deduct this missing bit of information by themselves. In addition, the *Encoding* class was abstract, meaning that one of its subclasses had to be instantiated and used.

```
public void setMailStartEnd(EMailDocument email, int startX,
int startY, int endX, int endY) {
    email.setStartElement(new MailStartTag(
    new CursorBlockPosition(startX, startY)));
    email.setEndElement(new MailEndTag(
    new CursorBlockPosition(endX, endY)));

    email.setFormat(new UTF8Encoding());
}
```

Listing 4-6: Solution to task 2 (Java)

The Groovy part for this task was very similar, only the class names changed to fit the different domain, as can be seen in Listing 4-7. The abstract class in Groovy was the *LevelType* class.

```
public void configureLevel(def level, def startX,
    def startY, def goalX, def goalY) {
    level.setStart(new StartLevelField(
    new Position(startX, startY)));
    level.setGoal(new GoalLevelField(
    new Position(goalX, goalY)));

    level.setLevelKind(new DungeonLevelType());
}
```

Listing 4-7: Solution to task 11 (Groovy)

Tasks 3 and 12 – 6 Types to identify

The two tasks 3 and 12 were again tasks of the category where participants had to identify types and their necessary dependencies and put their instances together in the correct way. For the Java part, a *MailElement* subclass of type *OptionalHeaderTag* had to be created, along with a header and a set of other dependencies, and then returned. The number of types to identify was 6 in this task.

```
public MailElement intializeElement(int x_position, int y_position,
    char headerType) throws InvalidHeaderException {

    Header header = new Header(headerType);
    OptionalHeaderTag newTag = new OptionalHeaderTag(x_position,
    y_position, header);

    newTag.setElementInfo(new DataList<MetaData>());
    newTag.setCursor(new DefaultCursor(new MetaDataCache(),
    new MetaDataDisplay()));

    return newTag;
}
```

Listing 4-8: Solution to task 3 (Java)

The Groovy part was essentially the same again, only differing in the class names because of the domain, and of course Groovy lacking static type information in the workspace.

```
public def setUpLevelField(def x_position,
        def y_position, def trapType) throws
InvalidTrapSymbolException {

    def trap = new Trap(trapType);
    def trapField = new TrappedLevelField(x_position, y_position,
    trap);

    trapField.setItems(new GameList());
    trapField.setSubject(new Player(new Inventory(), new Body()));

    return trapField;
}
```

Listing 4-9: Solution to task 12 (Groovy)

4.5.4.4 Tasks 4 and 13 – Semantic Error

Both applications had a system of Commands (Groovy) or Jobs (Java) which represented certain interactions with the application and which were executed in order to complete certain things in the environment, like teleporting a player from one field to another. Tasks 4 and 13 had an error introduced which resulted in a wrong program behavior for the application.

The participants were given code that performed a simulated interaction with the application and also a consistency check after running the actual task logic which was to provide them with hints and a method of understanding what kind of error they had to deal with.

In case of the Java application, the simulated interaction was that a cursor reached the last element of an e-mail, which should normally result in a job of type *ChangeMailJob* to be created and executed so that the next mail in the list is loaded. In this case, the wrong job type *SetCursorJob* was used to reset the cursor back to the first element of the current mail, being a wrong behavior (see Listing 4-10). The consistency check thus provided the participants with the error description, that the current document had not changed after reaching the last element.

```
protected void doCursorOnInteraction() {
    if (cursorOnElement instanceof DefaultCursor) {
        Job job = new SetCursorJob(cursorOnElement,
        MailEditorServer.getInstance().getCurrentDocument(), 0, 0);
        MailEditorServer.getInstance().addToActions(job);
    }
}
```

Listing 4-10: The part of task 4 with the error that leads to wrong behavior

The participants had to find this part of the application and change the behavior so that it did the right thing, in this case switching to the next mail. For this they had to first understand the code that was provided and follow it to the point where the error originated, then change the class that gets instantiated to *ChangeMailJob* and provide it with the necessary parameters. The needed parameter was the current field the interaction was executed on (the "this"-reference). Listing 4-11 and Listing 4-12 show the solutions for both parts.

```
protected void doCursorOnInteraction() {
    if (cursorOnElement instanceof DefaultCursor) {
        Job job = new ChangeMailJob(this);
        MailEditorServer.getInstance().addToActions(job);
    }
}
```

Listing 4-11: Solution to task 4 (Java)

```
protected def doMoveInteraction() {
    if (subjectOnField instanceof Player) {
        def command = new NextLevelCommand(this);
        GameManager.getInstance().queueCommand(command);
    }
}
```

Listing 4-12: Solution to task 13 (Groovy)

4.5.4.5 Tasks 5 and 14 – Semantic Error

Similar to tasks 4 and 13, the tasks 5 and 14 were semantic error tasks. Again, participants were provided with code that simulated an interaction with the application and did a consistency check as well. The point of tasks 4 and 13 was to find out that a call to a specific method was missing in the code, leading to unexpected behavior which would be found by the consistency check that then threw an exception.

To take the groovy part as an example this time, the domain problem was that once a player moved from one field of the level to the next, the execution of a move command should include setting the player reference to the new field as well as delete it from the old. In case of the semantic error introduced, the call which removed the reference from the old field was now missing, leading to a duplicate player reference on the game board. The code part the participants needed to find did first try to set the player on the field and then would do subsequent work in case setting the reference worked.

Listing 4-13 shows the mentioned part of the code. After successfully setting the reference, the position values are changed and an interaction is triggered. The missing call to remove the old reference had to be inserted inside this code block.

```
if (newField.setSubject(subject))
{
    subject.setPosition(newField.getX_position(),
    newField.getY_position());
    newField.subjectInteraction(InteractionType.Move);
}
```

Listing 4-13: Part of code from task 14 with missing line to remove reference

In the Java part's domain model, it was a cursor whose reference had to be removed from the old mail element that it pointed to before its moving. Everything else was similar. The solutions to both parts are presented here:

```
if (newField.setSubject(subject))
{
    subject.setPosition(newField.getX_position(),
    newField.getY_position());
    newField.subjectInteraction(InteractionType.Move);
    oldField.removeSubject();
}
```

Listing 4-14: Solution to task 14 (Groovy)

As with the previous task, the hardest part was to understand the error message of the consistency check and after figuring out what is going wrong finding the right place in the code to correct.

```
if (newElement.setCursor(cursor))
{
    cursor.setPosition(newElement.getX_position(),
    newElement.getY_position());
    newElement.interaction(MailAction.CursorOn);
    oldElement.removeCursor();
}
```

Listing 4-15: Solution to task 5 (Java)

4.5.4.6 Tasks 6 and 15 - 8 Types to identify

8 types had to be identified in tasks 6 and 15. For the Java application, the task was creating a new subclass of the *Cursor* class, the *WindowsMousePointer* class, which contained some simulated dependencies to classes like a *Theme* or *CursorFeatures*, representing icons that are shown as the pointer during loading and other features commonly associated with cursor behavior.

Another feature of this task was that it contained some subclassing logic, which forced the participants to identify a few class hierarchies and find the necessary subclass for the task, as well as enumeration types. For the enumeration types, it was not relevant which actual value the participants chose.

```
public Cursor createPointer() throws InvalidHeaderException {

    WorkInProgressPresentation progressRep = new
DefaultWorkInProgressPresentation(Animation.HourGlass);
    CursorFeatures features = new CursorFeatures(progressRep, new
IdleRepresentation());
    Theme theme = new Theme(new ThemeLocator());
    WindowsMousePointer pointer = new WindowsMousePointer(features,
theme);
    pointer.setTipOfDayPopup(new ShowTipEventManager());
    return pointer;
}
```

Listing 4-16: Solution to task 6 (Java)

For the task 15, the Groovy domain model required the participants to create a new actor for the game, which was not to be another player, but a monster, which had dependencies to attributes like the monster type, the damage type it deals or its resistances. Without further explanation, the Groovy solution is shown in Listing 4-17.

```
public def createNewActorForGame() throws InvalidTrapSymbolException {
    def attackType = new UnarmedAttackType(DamageType.default);
    def attributes = new SubjectAttributes(attackType, new
Resistances());
    def monster = new HillGiant(attributes, new Intrinsics(), new
Giants());
    monster.setDroppableItemGenerator(new RandomItemBuilder());
    return monster;
}
```

Listing 4-17: Solution to task 15 (Groovy)

4.5.4.7 Tasks 7 and 16 – Stack size 2 and branch size 3

Tasks 7 and 16 were tasks which contained latent type errors. As explained above, this means that the point at which a wrong type is passed as a parameter is at a different part of the program stack. In this case, the participants were given a simulated interaction with the application that created the wrong application state, along with some consistency check logic which was supposed to call the code which would use the wrong state and result in a type error during runtime for Groovy, or a compile error for Java.

Because the Groovy part is the most interesting for these type of tasks, all explanations will be done using the Groovy application. The code in Listing 4-18 shows the simulated interaction given to the participants in the task. The code essentially just calls the *TrapFactory* class to create a new trap, and then passes this instance to a new *TrappedLevelField*. This field is then queried in a consistency check which gets all messages of the trap on the field and checks whether they contain a specific word.

```
public def createNewTrappedFieldAndCheckIt(def x, def y,
        def trapType) throws InvalidTrapSymbolException {

    def newTrap = TrapFactory.createTrap(trapType);
    def newField = new TrappedLevelField(x, y, trapType, newTrap);

    def testPlayer = new Player();

    //Test if trap has correct values:
    if(newField.getTrap().getDetectedMessage(testPlayer)
    .contains("found") &&
    newField.getTrap().getDisarmedMessage(testPlayer)
    .contains("disarmed") &&
    newField.getTrap().getDodgedMessage(testPlayer)
    .contains("managed") &&
    newField.getTrap().getHitByTrapMessage(testPlayer)
    .contains("hit") &&
    newField.getTrap().getDamage() > 0)
        return newField;
    else
        return null;
}
```

Listing 4-18: The simulated interaction of task 16 (Groovy)

The error that is introduced in the logic following the *createTrap* call results in an object of a wrong type being put in to the *"HitByTrapMessage"* field, which again results in a runtime error as soon as the logic tries to concatenate this message with the player name. The wrong object in the field does not possess the *concat*-Method, because it is expected to be of type *String*. The part of the code responsible for inserting the wrong class is in the *createDartTrapProperties*-Method of the *TrapFactory*:

```
private static def createDartTrapProperties(def symbol) {

    def dartTrapProperties = new TrapProperties(
        8, String.valueOf(symbol), 1, 5, 9);

    dartTrapProperties.setDetectedMessage("found a dart trap.");
    dartTrapProperties.setDodgedMessage("managed to escape a dart
trap.");
    dartTrapProperties.setDisarmedMessage("disarmed a dart trap.");
    dartTrapProperties.setHitByTrapMessage(new GameObject(symbol,
"hit by a dart trap", 10)));
    dartTrapProperties.setVisible(false);

    return dartTrapProperties;
}
```

Listing 4-19: Point of bug insertion for task 16

When calling the *setHitByTrapMessage*-Method, it inserts a *GameObject* instance instead of just a *String*. Now, during the consistency check, the following happens in the corresponding *get*-Method:

```
public def getHitByTrapMessage(def subject) {
def message = myProperties.getHitByTrapMessage().concat(" " +
subject.getName());
    return message;
}
```

Listing 4-20: Point where bug results in runtime error for task 16

The method gets the message from the *TrapProperties* dependency object and tries to concatenate it with the name of the subject instance that is passed to the call. As the object in the property is of type *GameObject*, which does not possess the *concat*-Method, it results in a runtime Error.

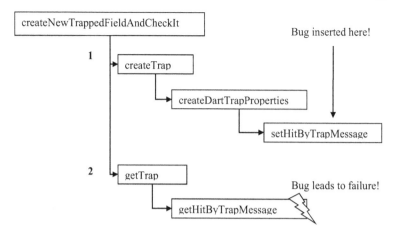

Figure 4-5: Simplified call stack containing bug creation and runtime error for task 16

In Figure 4-5, both branches of the simulated interaction are shown which lead to the runtime error. The branch labeled number one is the branch where the bug is created, and branch number two leads to the runtime error. This runtime error was easily removed, once found, by removing the *GameObject* instance from the logic that initializes the new *TrapProperties* and just putting only the *String* into the call. So the bulk of the work in the Groovy version of this task was supposed to be the search for the error source.

4.5.4.8 Tasks 8 and 17 – 12 types to identify

The two tasks 8 and 17 were the last of the type identification tasks, and also the two largest, as all in all 12 types had to be identified and put together in an object graph of instances.

In the Java part, the task was to configure a *MailAccount* class with a variety of dependent classes, each representing an aspect of mail account configuration, like a *MailInServer* or a *SendMailServer*, *UserCredentials* and more, including two *enum* types. Some of these classes again could also have dependencies to others, which had to be fulfilled, too. Except in one case, all dependencies had to be resolved using the given constructors of the classes. They had to be set using a method only once, as shown in the line next to the *return* statement.

```
public MailAccount createNewUserPrincipalAndAccount(String userName,
String password) {

    MailFormatter mailDOMCreator = new MailFormatter();
    MailFormatReader rawFileInputReader = new MailFormatReader();
    MailReader mailParser = new MailReader(mailDOMCreator,
rawFileInputReader);

    MailInServer incomingServer = new
MailInServer(EncryptionType.TLS, ServerType.IMAP);
    SendMailServer outgoingServer = new
SendMailServer(EncryptionType.TLS);
    ServerConfiguration serverData = new
ServerConfiguration(incomingServer, outgoingServer);

    LocalArchive mailLocation = new LocalArchive();
    Credentials loginInfo = new Credentials(userName, password);
    MailAccount result = new MailAccount(mailParser, serverData,
mailLocation, loginInfo);

    UserInfo userProfile = new UserInfo();
    result.setUserProfile(userProfile);
    return result;
}
```

Listing 4-21: Solution to task 8 (Java)

As with the other similar tasks, these classes were distributed throughout a few packages. The plan was to have these two tasks to contain the hugest amount of search effort from the participants. Listing 4-21 shows the rather large solution code for the Java part of this task. It can be seen very clearly that the dependencies were nested up to a total depth of three levels.

```
public def createPrototypeNetworkFunctionality() throws Exception {
    def pastEvents = new EventHistory();
    def incidentManager = new NetworkEventHandler(pastEvents);

    def transmissionMethod = TransportProtocol.TCP;
    def endPoint = new IPAddress();
    def serverFacade = new ServerProxy(transmissionMethod,
endPoint);

    def io = new FileAccess();
    def parser = new GameLevelParser();
    def formatter = new Serializer(io, parser);

    def result = new NetworkAccess(incidentManager, serverFacade,
formatter);

    def gameInfo = new GameData(GameState.Idle);
    result.setNextContent(new GamePackage(gameInfo));

    return result;
}
```

Listing 4-22: Solution to task 17 (Groovy)

For task 17, the Groovy part, the task required the participants to create a network configuration for the application which was represented by numerous classes, like *ServerProxy*, *IPAddress*, *GameData* and *NetworkEventHandler*, among others. Again, two *enum* types were needed and the depth of the nesting went up to three, too.

4.5.4.9 Tasks 9 and 18 – Stack size 2 and branch size 5

Being the last tasks for both parts, tasks 9 and 18 were also designed to be among the more difficult tasks. In Java however, this error would be detected by the compiler, making it actually fairly easy to fix. But, for the Groovy part, task 18 could be considered to be the most difficult task of the whole experiment.

Similar to tasks 7 and 16, explanation of the task will only concentrate on the Groovy part in task 18.

What the participants were asked to do was to find an error in a simulated interaction with the application again. This time, the program failure was even farther removed from the actual bug insertion.

```
public def player3StepsRight() {
    tasksAndMessages.queueNewTask(CommandFactory.
                getMoveCommand(player, currentlevel,
MoveDirection.Right));
    tasksAndMessages.queueNewTask(CommandFactory.
                getMoveCommand(player, currentlevel,
MoveDirection.Right));
    tasksAndMessages.queueNewTask(CommandFactory.
                getMoveCommand(player, currentlevel,
MoveDirection.Right));
    tasksAndMessages.executeTasks();
}
```

Listing 4-23: Simulated interaction for task 18 (Groovy)

The Listing 4-23 shows the simulated interaction that was given to the participants. The first three statements only prepared the commands to be executed. The actual interaction was executed in the last method call *executeTasks*. The participants were also given an explanation of what that interaction represented: A player moved three steps to the right, and his last step would lead to a teleport trap being triggered that was supposed to be teleporting him somewhere.

The actual bug was introduced in the *CommandFactory* that was used to create the commands for execution:

```
public static def getTeleportCommand(def subject, def level, int x,
int y) {
    return new TeleportCommand(level, subject, x ,y);
}
```

Listing 4-24: Point of bug insertion for Task 18

The bug itself seems like a simple mistake, the parameters that were required by the *TeleportCommand* (a *GameSubject* and a *GameLevel* instance) were passed to the constructor in the wrong order, resulting in the level being saved as the subject and vice versa. This lead to a program error during runtime in Groovy, when the teleport logic tried to call a method for getting the game board on the *Player* instance that was in the subject variable.

```
public def evaluateTeleport() {

    def board = level.getGameBoard();
    if (x <= board.length && y <= board[x].length)
    {
        def newField = board[x][y];
        if (newField.setSubject(subject))
            subject.setPosition(x, y);
    }
}
```

Listing 4-25: Point where bug results in runtime Error for Task 18

Figure 4-6 shows the simplified call stack for the problem. The call to *executeTasks* at the end of the simulated interaction leads to the *doIt*-Method and subsequently the *evaluteMove* and *subjectInteraction* Methods of the three commands being called. But the last command's interaction results in the triggering of the teleport trap, which creates the new *TeleportCommand* via the *getTeleportCommand*-Method of the *CommandFactory* (which inserts the bug) and puts it into the command queue. So the next thing the *executeTasks*-Method does is evaluate that newly created *TeleportCommand*, leading to the runtime error.

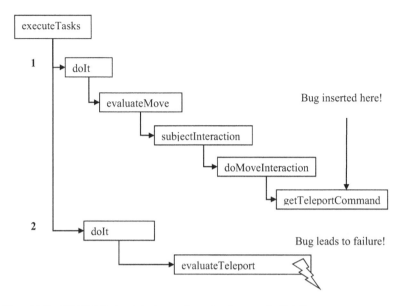

Figure 4-6: Simplified Call Stack containing bug creation and runtime error for Task 18

The resulting error message that Groovy returned was not easily interpreted, making this error very difficult to find, although it was essentially only misplaced constructor parameters. Another factor which increased the difficulty was the fact that the creation of the teleport interaction was a direct result of the last step the player made, and thus the call to *getTeleportCommand* was not included in the original interaction as seen in Listing 4-23. So to solve the problem, the participants had to find out why the error happened, then where. After the point had been found, a simple switching of the two parameters back to their correct order for the constructor did the trick to complete the task.

4.5.4.10 Summary of Variables and Mapping of Tasks to Hypotheses

After describing all tasks categories and the exact tasks, the independent variables and their mapping toward the hypotheses are summarized here. As already mentioned, the type identification tasks (1, 2, 3, 6 and 8) were primarily included for the main hypothesis, the semantic error tasks (4 and 5) for hypothesis 2-2 and the latent type error tasks (7 and 9) for hypothesis 2-1. Table 4-2 gives a short overview of the independent variables involved and which treatment values they had. The dependent variable of the whole experiment was time.

Independent Variable (IV)	IV Treatments	Tasks	Dependent Variable
Programming Language	Java / Groovy	All	Time
Number of Types to identify	2, 4, 6, 8 and 12	1, 2, 3, 6, 8	Time
Branch size	3 and 5	7, 9	Time

Table 4-2: Summary of the independent variables, their values, corresponding tasks and dependent variables

4.6 Experiment Implementation

The experiment implementation stretched across about six to eight weeks, during which participants were found by means of personal approach, entries in web boards and e-mailing (this method of acquiring participants is also called convenience sampling). No special difficulties were encountered, even though some small adaptations had to be made on the environment, none of which had any significant impact on the experiment's outcome and analysis.

In the end, a total of 36 participants had taken part in the experiment, of which 33 were able to finish all tasks (most of them were undergraduates, some graduates, and some practitioners, for a more detailed description of the participants see the appendix under A.2.6). The three participants that did not finish the experiment did so due to various reasons, these being -among others- lack of time or the necessary skill. This is still a very low mortality rate. Their incomplete datasets where discarded from the analysis, which is the reason why the participant numbering in the data is not in a straight sequence. Additionally, in tradition of programming using zero-indexed collections, participant numbering starts with a zero.

After the experiment, the log files were analyzed and the necessary data for analysis was extracted using a tool specifically written in Java for this task. The extracted times were measured in seconds while fractures of these seconds were simply cut off during the extraction process. This was done on the assumption that this small loss of precision can be neglected for such an experiment.

5. Threats to Validity

This chapter explains and discusses several threats that can harm the validity of the experiment.

Validity in controlled experiments is split into internal and external validity. Internal validity refers to the extent of control over the unsystematic variation, meaning how well the random "noise" and other undesired influences were kept to a minimum. In other words, internal validity is high if the changes in the dependent variable can be specifically linked to the manipulation of the independent variables. External validity on the other hand, refers to the extent to which the experiments results are generalizable to other situations. It is influenced for example by using only a specific type of person in the experiment (only professionals for example), because then the results are probably not reliable and would be different when repeating the experiment with a different group of persons.

5.1 Internal Validity

Learning and practice effects: Some of the major threats to internal validity are learning and practice effects that appear between measuring different experiment conditions with the same participants. These are especially important in skill-oriented experiments like this one where a huge learning effect can lead to completely useless experiment results. Some measures besides the inherent experiment design were taken to minimize learning effects, namely first the complete renaming/modification of code artifacts and thus changing the application domain while leaving the underlying code structure intact (which in itself could have introduced a new variable: The understandability of the used domain/application). Second the sequential numbering of the tasks (1 through 18 instead of Java/Groovy 1 through 9), the task choice and order (putting semantic error tasks between type identification tasks to reduce concentration of learning effects on one task type) and the attempt to not include too important parts of code for later tasks in earlier tasks. The latter measure could only be taken to a small extent, because some parts of the application could not be removed in earlier tasks (there were functional dependencies) even though they were possibly needed in later tasks. This could have had the result that some participants found relevant parts of a task while searching in a completely wrong part of the code of another task.

Participant variance and human factors: A second possibly major threat to internal validity is the variance between the participants. Some were probably very good developers, some average, some novices, and their experience with the involved programming languages differed surely (although Groovy is still a relatively new language, some could have used it before and Groovy experience was erroneously not included in the questionnaire). It is very obvious that this would have had a big impact on individual results and the overall experiment, especially when no real estimation and classification of their skills was possible. But the Groovy part of the experiment was more or less just a dynamically typed Java, so differences because of language knowledge should have been minimal. Another measure taken against participant variance was the alternating (and thus pseudo-random) order in which participants were put into the two groups. Additionally, some participants might not have been in best shape or mood for the experiment (some said they had attended exams right before the experiment, some did not have the time to complete the experiment on one day and had to finish on another). These and many more "human factors" can be sources of unsystematic variation and controlling all of this "noise" is certainly impossible.

Environment, IDE: Also, there possibly were differences in the way the participants got familiar with the environment and IDE. Some participated in other experiments using the same environment, thus benefitting from this experience. Others were new to the IDE and might have taken longer to get accustomed to it.

Tasks: Even the tasks themselves could be a source of variance, i.e. they did not simply differ in terms of number of types to identify, but each had its own small problem domain that might have had an impact on the results. Some participants took longer before they grasped the task and some had to ask questions (which was legitimate and they were even told to ask questions early instead of brooding over task understanding alone too long). Consequently, the time measured is definitely not the pure time needed for the participants to solve the task from a simple work aspect, but also includes the time to get to know the classes and understand the task. Besides, the participants also did not have the choice on how to solve the tasks but were more or less forced to solve it in the way the tests demanded.

5.2 External Validity

IDE: One problem that reduces external validity is the used IDE. Its rather poor set of features and usability are nothing compared to the support of powerful IDEs that are commonly used today. It did not even have a debugger and suffered from sporadic bugs. Many developers are used to these powerful features so much that they are seriously hampered in their work progress when using such an archaic tool.

Application and Tasks: The tasks and the applications themselves are discussable, too. While the application's structure, architecture and design were quite close to those of many other small software systems, they were modified to cater for the needs of the experiment and thus did not actually represent a totally authentic code base but only very abstract versions of realistic coding scenarios. This might raise a lot of doubt as to the transferability of the results to so-called real situations or even other experiments. But despite these objections, comparability can still be good with similarly designed experiments. In addition, software development tasks seldom only consist of just programming but also design and other choices which were completely neglected here.

Undocumented API and variable naming: While having to use an uncommented API might not be very uncommon, the naming of the variables used in the experiment was. This is especially important when using the results to compare the two languages via their performance. Variables that are not named to exactly represent the type of the content they contain make programming in a dynamically typed language very hard. It can thus be argued that the experiment design itself was in favor of the static type systems, as any good dynamic type system programmer would probably make sure to name any variables accordingly. On the other hand, modern IDEs can also provide context-sensitive support in dynamically typed languages, too. And programmers in statically typed languages are encouraged to use meaningful variable names even though they can rely on the type system. Nevertheless, the assumption of the experiment was a completely undocumented API, and undocumented also includes the documentation value of method and variable names (hence the obfuscation of the important variables). But this would mean that a next step could be a comparison with an API that is not obfuscated.

Students as subjects: Another threat is the fact that the participants consisted mainly of students. Hence, it is questionable whether a study with more experienced professional developers would have yielded different results. Some of these doubts have already been raised by others and some related work was mentioned and discussed on the topic. The conclusion remains the same: Even if students might differ in general performance from industry developers (who might solve tasks in a faster absolute time), what was most important was to analyze the within-subject differences between the two parts. So, even if an industry developer had solved the complete experiment faster, the relation between the two parts is very probably similar to those of the students. And it should be mentioned, that all of the fastest participants in the study have been students.

Negligible Difference of Programming Language Syntax: Finally, the last detail worth considering: Java and Groovy (at least the way Groovy was used in this experiment) differ only by their type systems; all other syntax features that were used in the experiment were similar. A good Java developer would therefore have benefitted from his skill even when he did not know Groovy before and had to start with the Groovy part. This could mean that even if all developers had never used Groovy before, good Java developers would have had an advantage over others no matter which language they started with. At this university, Java is the main teaching language and industry developers as well as research associates are commonly well-versed in its use. A developer with a non-Java background might produce completely different results. If this effect in fact occurred in the experiment is only speculative.

In general, the artificial environment created for controlled experiments is always a big threat to their validity but it is a necessary tradeoff between external validity and their exact results for specific questions.

6. Analysis and Results

As a next step, the data gathered in the experiment is analyzed using different approaches and statistical tests. Some more information on the statistical tests and methods used can be found in the appendix (A.1), but most are fairly common. Because the distinction of the tasks 1 through 9 and 10 to 18 was only artificially introduced, the tasks are now only numbered from 1 through 9 and referred to in this way. Time is unless otherwise stated measured in seconds. Sometimes the two groups are just referred to as GS or JS (Groovy starters or Java starters) and the tasks abbreviated with a Gx or Jx (for Groovy or Java and x for the task number).

The first part of this chapter is formed by some descriptive statistics on the overall data, followed by the main part of the analysis. The main part consists of different analyses done on the data: A within-subject analysis of the overall experiment results, an analysis for residual (sequence or carry-over) effects in the data, which leads to the conclusion that using the overall data as analysis base might be problematic. This is then followed by a within-subject analysis inside the two groups (Java/Groovy starters), an exploratory analysis of the results based on the best/worst scoring participants and a hypothesis based analysis of the specific task types.

6.1 General Descriptive Statistics

In this part, some measures and variants of descriptive statistics along with their respective diagrams of the data are presented. The raw data of all participant times can be found in the appendix (A.2) for reference.

The boxplot in Figure 6-1 shows the result distribution of the times of all participants for all tasks in the experiment. The one thing that sticks out is that there seems to be a huge number of outliers and even quite a few extremes in the data. This phenomenon is not restricted to any special task. Another fact that might be worth mentioning is that the top whiskers of quite a few tasks are longer than the bottom ones, meaning that the quartile containing the slowest 25% of participants for a task has a much higher variability in the values. This makes some of the distributions very asymmetrical.

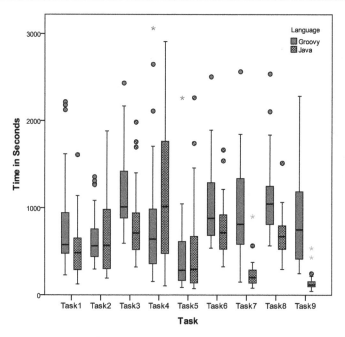

Figure 6-1: Boxplot of complete experiment results

The next step is to have a look at some descriptive statistics data on the results shown above:

Task	G1	G2	G3	G4	G5	G6	G7	G8	G9
Median	575	562	1010	639	282	880	813	1046	750
Mean	818	669	1182	814	429	1026	928	1112	849
Min.	227	295	591	153	87	537	149	564	246
Max.	2215	1354	2433	3062	2262	2505	2565	2538	2285
Std. Dev.	552	309	453	696	426	461	549	417	557

Table 6-1: Descriptive statistics data of Groovy tasks for all participants (in seconds)

Task	J1	J2	J3	J4	J5	J6	J7	J8	J9
Median	480	567	711	1015	293	716	197	671	116
Mean	535	781	813	1111	507	827	236	691	147
Min.	124	193	320	104	74	323	78	293	44
Max.	1609	4285	1983	2910	2264	3240	900	1514	535
Std. Dev.	336	787	410	798	528	543	159	246	101

Table 6-2: Descriptive statistics data of Java tasks for all participants (in seconds)

	Median	Mean	Minimum	Maximum	Standard Derivation
Total Time	13469	13475	6462	28971	4556

Table 6-3: Descriptive statistics data of total experiment time for all participants (in seconds)

The numbers confirm the picture given by the boxplot. There is a high variability in the values, which can be easily seen by having a look at the minimum and maximum values for each task and also the total time. There are huge differences. The total time can serve as an example: The fastest participant needed approximately one hour and 45 minutes for the whole experiment, while the slowest needed about eight hours in total. Median and mean being also quite a few steps apart for many tasks (like G1 or G5) confirms this.

Tasks 7 and 9 display the expected results: Java seems to outperform Groovy. Tasks 4 and 5 seem to display results going in two directions, one in favor of Java and one for Groovy. This has to be examined in more detail to make any useful statement. The means of the type identification tasks are slightly larger for Groovy in most tasks. Tests need to be done whether there is a significant difference.

6.2 Statistical Tests and Analysis

The normal procedure when statistically analyzing data is to first check whether they are normally distributed. That means using the Kolmogorov-Smirnov (K-S) and Shapiro-Wilk (S-W) tests on them, both of which are explained in more detail in the appendix (in A.1 along with all other statistical tests). Here it should suffice to say that they can be used to check whether a given amount of data can be assumed to come from a normally distributed set, which is an important assumption needed for the follow-up tests that are used to check for statistically significant differences in the data. In case a set of data is normally distributed, a t-test can be used to test for significance. In the case of a non-normally distributed set, the Wilcoxon-Test can be used.

6.2.1 Within-Subject Analysis on the complete data

The first analysis that was done was a within-subject analysis of the task times for all participants, comparing the times of the respective Java task to its corresponding Groovy task, to see if there is a significant difference between the two. The analysis does not differentiate between participants that started with Java or Groovy; it just takes all values into consideration. This is rather problematic because it neglects any learning or practice effects. It is still useful to check because it can tell if there is any difference between the times at all.

In many cases it is said that a normal-distribution can be assumed if the set of data is larger than about 30 entries. The tests were still run on the data with surprising results, as displayed in Table 6-4.

	Kolmogorov-Smirnov[a]			Shapiro-Wilk		
	Statistic	df	Sig.	Statistic	df	Sig.
Task1	.114	33	.200	.946	33	.103
Task2	.200	33	.002	.680	33	.000
Task3	.133	33	.149	.967	33	.391
Task4	.134	33	.144	.960	33	.266
Task5	.168	33	.019	.926	33	.026
Task6	.134	33	.137	.937	33	.057
Task7	.100	33	.200	.952	33	.151
Task8	.194	33	.003	.895	33	.004
Task9	.164	33	.025	.882	33	.002

a. Lilliefors Significance Correction

*. This is a lower bound of the true significance.

Table 6-4: Results of the tests for normal-distribution for the complete data, comparing task differences based on the language used

The K-S says that only the differences of scores for tasks 1, 3, 4, 6 and 7 are normally-distributed (significance values greater than 0.05). The S-W test (which is considered more powerful) confirms this. A look at the histograms (which were omitted here) confirmed the test results, some of the distributions look far from being normally-distributed, some come pretty close. So, According to S-W, the application of the dependent t-test does make sense on the mentioned tasks. The results tell us that there is a significant difference between the Groovy and Java results for tasks 1, 3 and 7. In addition, the other tasks are analyzed using the Wilcoxon Signed Rank Test (the tasks already analyzed using the t-test are included for completion and comparison) and in case of significance the dominating group is marked (meaning group with faster times).

	J1 - G1	J2 - G2	J3 - G3	J4 - G4	J5 - G5	J6 - G6	J7 - G7	J8 - G8	J9 - G9
t-test Sig. (2-tailed)	.002	-	.001	.092	-	.076	.000	-	-
Exact Sig. (2-tailed)	.003	.884	.001	.130	.560	.027	.000	.000	.000
Dominating Ranks	Java	-	Java	-	-	Java	Java	Java	Java

Table 6-5: Results of the t-test and Wilcoxon Signed Rank tests on the complete data, comparing tasks based on the language used

For the semantic error tasks 4 and 5 these seem like good results, as there is no significant difference between the two languages, supporting the 2-2 hypothesis (no difference in needed time for fixing semantic errors no matter the type system). The results for the type identification tasks are (except for task 2 where the result is not significant in both tests) in favor of the static type system, as the results are based on positive ranks, indicating that more participants solved the task faster with Java. It should be noted though, that the two tests provide contradicting results for task 6. This might be because with a p score of 0.057 in the S-W test, the data barely qualifies for the t-test and its results might be biased because of this close call. Not surprising at all are the results for the two tasks 7 and 9, were the Java compiler pointed out the error and lead to quick completion.

However, all these results are very raw and do not consider any learning- or other effects. So before drawing any conclusions yet, the next step would be to check whether the grouping actually had a significant impact on the results and whether the within-subject analysis for the two separate groups yields significant results.

6.2.2 Analysis for residual effects between the two Participant Groups

In repeated-measures experiments, participants are subjected to manipulation from the experimenter on all experimental conditions because they participate in all parts of the experiment. When trying to be very specific, these conditions were the nine tasks and two languages in this experiment. To have valid results in the end, it is very important to make the right analyses on the right sets of data. Until now, only the whole data was inspected. This approach is not entirely correct without checking some pre-requisites first. It is imperative to know whether the blocking did have a significant impact on the results for the tasks, based on which of the two was the starting language. An effect like this is called a carry-over or residual effect. [Jones and Kenward 1989] give a whole chapter dedicated to handling this effect (page 39 pp.), but as knowledge about experimental design and using appropriate statistical methods is still almost non-existent in software engineering, it is not entirely clear how to proceed in this specific situation.

One reasonable approach is to compare the specific parts between the two groups; this means comparing the Java times of the Java starters to the Java times of the Groovy starters and vice-versa. If these values actually differ significantly between the groups, it is clear that there must be some kind of effect hidden, which is most probably a residual learning effect. This would mean that it makes a difference with which language a participant started and therefore all results cannot be analyzed as one set, but only in between the two groups.

Hence, a statistical test for independent samples needs to be used. One is the independent t-test, which has the assumption of normally-distributed data, which is the first thing to test. The results are contained in the appendix (Table A-5) and they show that only the pairings of Java task 1 (barely) and Groovy task 7 qualify for the t-test. Because only these two tests qualify and one of them barely escaped a significant difference from normal distribution (it has a p-value of 0.057), the t-test will not be used, but the Mann-Whitney-U and Kolmogorov-Smirnov-Z non-parametric tests instead.

	J1	J2	J3	J4	J5	J6	J7	J8	J9
MW-U Exact Sig. (2-tailed)	.000	.000	.000	.000	.000	.000	.005	.000	.038
KS-Z Exact Sig. (2-tailed)	.000	.000	.000	.000	.001	.000	.012	.000	.022
Dominating Ranks	GS	GS	GS	GS	GS	GS	GS	GS	GS

Table 6-6: Results of the Mann-Whitney-U and Kolmogorov-Smirnov-Z test when comparing Java task results between Groups (GS=GroovyStarters)

The result for the Java tasks is very apparent. There is a strong significant difference between the two groups for the Java tasks, with the Groovy starter group dominating in every case. This hardens the assumption that the Groovy Starters would benefit from both the learning effect and the type system in Java making the tasks easier. But it could also mean that the chosen domain for the Java part made it easier to understand the application. Now, on to the results for the Groovy tasks:

	G1	G2	G3	G4	G5	G6	G7	G8	G9
MW-U Exact Sig. (2-tailed)	.575	.783	.127	.009	.058	.657	.191	.110	.631
KS-Z Exact Sig. (2-tailed)	.836	.574	.118	.039	.014	.686	.323	.096	.891
Dominating Ranks	-	-	-	JS	JS	-	-	-	-

Table 6-7: Results of the Mann-Whitney-U and Kolmogorov-Smirnov-Z test when comparing Groovy task results between Groups (JS = JavaStarters)

The results are very different for the Groovy part, where there are only two tasks where there is a significant difference between the groups. These are task 4 (U-test and the KS-Z test) and task 5 (only KS-Z), the semantic error tasks, both dominated by the Java starters (very probably due to a learning effect for this task type). This means for the Groovy tasks that it either did not matter which language a participant started with, or more probably that the learning effect of the participants that started with Java was canceled out by the additional difficulty that was introduced by the language.

This also leads to the conclusion that there is some kind of residual learning effect and that analyzing the samples as one set of data would produce inaccurate results. Consequently, from now on, the two groups that started with different languages need to be analyzed separately from each other.

6.2.3 Within-Subject Analysis on the two Participant Groups

After splitting the complete results into the two groups that started with different languages, the first meaningful thing to do is to have a look at some descriptive statistics of the two groups' scores. After testing for normal-distribution, either a t-test or Wilcoxon-test can be used to show if the differences in the two language parts are significant. This is done separately for each group.

6.2.3.1 Participants that started with Groovy

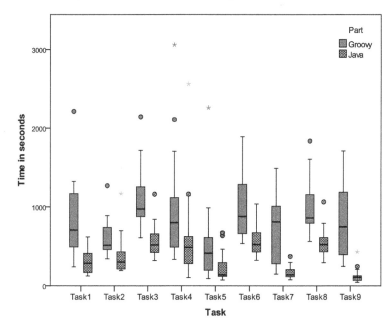

Figure 6-2: Boxplot of results for the Groovy starter group

One can see from the distribution of the data in Figure 6-2, that the first part (Groovy) has a much higher variance and means, while having a stronger spread in the top and lower 25% quantils. The Java part in comparison has lower medians and much less variance. In this case, the picture is pretty clear, and the descriptive data confirm it.

Task	G1	G2	G3	G4	G5	G6	G7	G8	G9
Median	709	516	976	801	416	880	813	862	750
Mean	822	616	1074	1022	539	992	758	1004	788
Min.	241	345	611	337	92	537	149	564	246
Max.	2215	1273	2146	3062	2262	1894	1492	1838	1712
Std. Dev.	491	233	386	726	510	412	436	326	472

Table 6-8: Descriptive statistics of Groovy tasks for participants that started with Groovy (in seconds)

Task	J1	J2	J3	J4	J5	J6	J7	J8	J9
Median	288	301	520	489	139	526	139	526	106
Mean	322	391	570	639	237	565	173	552	127
Min.	124	193	320	104	74	323	78	293	44
Max.	621	1169	1163	2562	673	1039	374	1064	430
Std. Dev.	150	256	210	592	194	201	82	182	95

Table 6-9: Descriptive statistics of Java tasks for participants that started with Groovy (in seconds)

	Median	Mean	Minimum	Maximum	Standard Derivation
Total Time	9753	11192	6462	16905	3191

Table 6-10: Descriptive statistics of total time for participants that started with Groovy (in seconds)

From the data and boxplot it seems that the Groovy-Starters mostly have a much lower mean/median score for all of the Java tasks. This observation strongly supports hypothesis 1. The exceptionally huge difference in times might additionally come from the fact that either most Groovy-starters were exceptionally experienced developers in Java or from a strong learning effect between the two parts (at least for this group). The latter seems to be a more likely explanation, but there will be more talk about this later.

Another fact worth mentioning is that when plotting histograms of the data one discovers that almost all of them display a positively skewed distribution (meaning many values cluster on the left side of the histogram). The middle part which should be largest in a normal distribution is considerably underrepresented. Figure 6-3 is included as an example of one of these distributions.

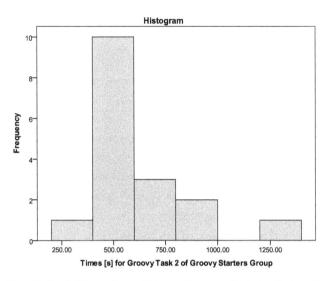

Figure 6-3: Sample histogram for a positively skewed frequency distribution of task results

Statistical tests should show whether these results are significant. But first, it is imperative to check again whether the data fulfill the t-test assumption, so the tests for normal-distribution are applied.

	Kolmogorov-Smirnov[a]			Shapiro-Wilk		
	Statistics	df	Sig.	Statistics	df	Sig.
Task1	.209	15	.077	.833	15	.010
Task2	.122	15	.200*	.958	15	.665
Task3	.214	15	.063	.930	15	.276
Task4	.134	15	.200*	.959	15	.669
Task5	.197	15	.123	.846	15	.015
Task6	.249	15	.013	.910	15	.134
Task7	.193	15	.139	.903	15	.105
Task8	.253	15	.011	.797	15	.003
Task9	.227	15	.037	.879	15	.045

a. Lilliefors Significance Correction

*. This is a lower bound of the true significance.

Table 6-11: Results of the tests for normal-distribution for the Groovy starter group, comparing task time differences based on the language used

And as the evaluation of the differences for the tasks shows, the differences for tasks 2, 3, 4, 6, and 7 can be assumed to be normally-distributed and qualify for the t-test. The Wilcoxon test is also applied to all tasks again. The t-test discovers that the results for all qualifying tasks are significantly different (p < 0.05), which is also confirmed by the Wilcoxon-test, which detects significant differences for all other tasks.

	J1 - G1	J2 - G2	J3 - G3	J4 - G4	J5 - G5	J6 - G6	J7 - G7	J8 - G8	J9 - G9
t-test Sig. (2-tailed)	-	.000	.000	.036	-	.000	.000	-	-
Exact Sig. (2-tailed)	.000	.000	.000	.027	.027	.000	.000	.000	.000
Dominating Ranks	Java	Java	Java	Java	Java	Java	Java	Java	Java

Table 6-12: Results of the t-test and Wilcoxon-test for the Groovy starter group

The dominating (in other terms, "faster") language in the comparison was always Java in this case. So, it can be stated with strong confidence that there is a significant difference between all the task results of the part the participants started with (in this case Groovy), and the repeated-measure part. In almost all cases (derived from rank results) they were significantly faster than in the first part. These findings are strongly supporting hypothesis 1. Even if a learning effect is considered to be part of the equation, the two effects simply add up to display such a huge difference in the scores.

The results of the type identification tasks are the most interesting considering hypothesis 1, although the overall results would have to be interpreted later when looking at the results of the Java starters group. The tasks 7 and 9 display results that could have been expected, while Tasks 4 and 5 show a surprisingly large difference between the parts, even if by hypothesis 2-2 similar times would have been expected. This could be due to the learning effect being especially strong here, remembering that these tasks were semantic errors that could be solved easily when the bug location was known, and participants might have recognized the similarities between the tasks in both parts, which would have lead them to the error rather quickly.

6.2.3.2 Participants that started with Java

For the Java starter group, the picture does not seem as clear as for the Groovy starters. As can be seen in Figure 6-4, not in all cases did the first part take a longer time. The obvious results for tasks 7 and 9 can be ignored for now. For tasks 4 and 5, the results are similar to the Groovy starter group, as the second part was solved a lot faster. This could again be the effect of learning because they might have remembered that the task had a similar solution during the first part.

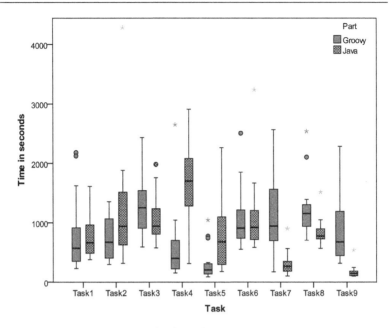

Figure 6-4: Boxplot of results for the Java starter group

Task	G1	G2	G3	G4	G5	G6	G7	G8	G9
Median	569	673	1252	397	205	908	945	1154	673
Mean	812	726	1298	592	312	1062	1109	1227	914
Min.	227	295	591	153	87	549	170	703	315
Max.	2179	1354	2433	2648	1045	2505	2565	2538	2285
Std. Dev.	626	373	502	607	284	519	611	480	645

Table 6-13: Descriptive statistics of Groovy tasks for participants that started with Java (in seconds)

Task	J1	J2	J3	J4	J5	J6	J7	J8	J9
Median	662	938	940	1703	678	918	263	777	145
Mean	762	1195	1070	1614	794	1106	303	838	168
Min.	375	315	574	312	177	582	102	566	98
Max.	1609	4285	1983	2910	2264	3240	900	1514	535
Std. Dev.	331	948	417	679	621	652	193	221	107

Table 6-14: Descriptive statistics of Java tasks for participants that started with Java (in seconds)

	Median	Mean	Minimum	Maximum	Standard Derivation
Total Time	15702	15902	9663	28971	4607

Table 6-15: Descriptive statistics of total time for participants that started with Java (in seconds)

There are a few exceptions where the mean and median are larger for the repetition when compared to the first part. With the main hypothesis in mind, the results of the type identification tasks except for task 2 are encouraging, as they all display that more time was needed using Groovy, in spite of a learning effect that is very likely. Again, the necessary statistical tests are applied to check the results.

	Kolmogorov-Smirnov[a]			Shapiro-Wilk		
	Statistics	df	Sig.	Statistics	df	Sig.
Task1	.167	15	.200	.910	15	.136
Task2	.243	15	.018	.769	15	.001
Task3	.123	15	.200	.973	15	.897
Task4	.194	15	.135	.897	15	.084
Task5	.246	15	.015	.858	15	.023
Task6	.249	15	.013	.907	15	.120
Task7	.139	15	.200	.950	15	.524
Task8	.150	15	.200	.940	15	.378
Task9	.187	15	.166	.886	15	.058

a. Lilliefors Significance Correction

*. This is a lower bound of the true significance.

Table 6-16: Results of the tests for normal-distribution for the Java starter group, comparing task time differences based on the language used

Use of the t-test is permitted on tasks 1, 3, 4, 6, 7, 8 and 9, but the Wilcoxon test is still applied to all of them for the useful rank results.

	J1 - G1	J2 - G2	J3 - G3	J4 - G4	J5 - G5	J6 - G6	J7 - G7	J8 - G8	J9 - G9
t-test Sig. (2-tailed)	.632	-	.207	.000	-	.822	.000	.004	.000
Exact Sig. (2-tailed)	.940	.034	.231	.000	.002	.706	.000	.002	.000
Dominating Ranks	-	Groovy	-	Groovy	Groovy	-	Java	Java	Java

Table 6-17: Results of the t-test and Wilcoxon-test for the Java starter group

The test results of this group and their possible implications require a more thorough explanation. But first, the obvious results for tasks 7 and 9 should be mentioned here shortly: They are significantly different for both tasks and in favor of Java, as expected.

More interesting are the results for tasks 4 and 5. Both t-test and Wilcoxon test confirm that there are significant differences between the results, and the rank number explicitly favors Groovy. This is the same situation as in the Groovy starters group, the second part was solved much faster. This strongly suggests that there is some kind of learning effect at work for these two tasks, as it is very unlikely that any other random factor would result in the second part being solved exceptionally faster for both groups.

The results for the type identification tasks 1, 2, 3, 6 and 8 have to be interpreted in the following way: Remembering hypothesis 1, it was stated that a static type system would lead to faster solving of programming tasks. This means, that either the participants of this group would actually take longer to solve the Groovy part, or at least need approximately the same amount of time (assuming the learning effect after solving the first part and the additional time needed to use the dynamically typed Groovy in the second part would roughly cancel each other out). The former is the case for task 8 (the largest with 12 types to identify), where the Java results are dominating and the results are strongly significant for both tests. The latter is the case for tasks 1, 3 and 6, where there is no statistically significant difference in the times. Both tests confirm the significance. Only task 2 (4 types had to be identified) displays a strange result: More participants solved it faster in the Groove part, this observation being even significant. This is an outlier and what might be the reason for this will be looked into later. Together with the findings from the Groovy starters group, the results are generally in favor of hypothesis 1.

6.2.4 Exploratory Analysis of the Results based on Participants' Performance

It is an interesting aspect of the experiment whether the results of participants that had an overall good performance in the experiment exhibit certain characteristics. Participants that scored well in the experiment are probably better developers in general. So it is interesting to see whether good developers score different in the experiment or benefit from the type system differently. Hence, the participants' two groups (Java and Groovy starters) are again split into two groups, using the total time needed for the whole experiment as the splitting factor[1]. The groups will be called outperformer group for the best 50% and underperformer for the other half. Splitting is done using the median, and in case of odd distributions the median value is included in the outperformer group. Thus, for Groovy starters, the distribution is now 9 participants in the outperformer group and 8 in the underperformer group. For Java starters, both groups are made up of 8 participants.

The same descriptive statistics and within-subject analysis methods already used above will be applied to the two performance groups for both language starter groups. All in

---

[1] There is also a part in the appendix where the performance is analysis is applied to the complete experiment data, included for sake of completeness (A.2.5).

all, there are four analyses to be done. The supplemental data in the appendix contains the results of the tests for normal distribution to save space (A.2.4).

6.2.4.1 Participants that started with Groovy

First displayed are the descriptive statistics of the outperformer group.

Task	G1	G2	G3	G4	G5	G6	G7	G8	G9
Median	563	497	904	747	358	685	308	812	636
Mean	588	529	928	701	306	785	626	794	784
Min.	241	345	611	358	92	537	149	564	273
Max.	1232	742	1371	1117	611	1621	1371	884	1571
Std. Dev.	290	126	215	281	170	332	485	94	472

Table 6-18: Descriptive statistics of Groovy tasks for outperformer participants that started with Groovy (in seconds)

Task	J1	J2	J3	J4	J5	J6	J7	J8	J9
Median	170	215	432	281	127	443	129	501	116
Mean	264	247	452	336	208	437	128	480	116
Min.	124	193	320	104	74	323	88	293	44
Max.	522	313	579	626	673	576	172	671	244
Std. Dev.	148	50	82	189	213	93	30	107	73

Table 6-19: Descriptive statistics of Java tasks for outperformer participants that started with Groovy (in seconds)

	Median	Mean	Minimum	Maximum	Standard Derivation
Total Time	8944	8706	6462	9753	975

Table 6-20: Descriptive statistics of total time for outperformer participants that started with Groovy (in seconds)

The data of the outperformer Groovy starter group seem much more homogenous than the data of all participants in that group as the standard deviation is generally lower for all tasks as well as for the total time. Next shown are the results of the significance analysis (tasks 2, 3, 4, 5, 8, and 9 have been tested to be normally distributed and qualify for the t-test, see appendix A.2.4) with both t-test and Wilcoxon test.

	J1 - G1	J2 - G2	J3 - G3	J4 - G4	J5 - G5	J6 - G6	J7 - G7	J8 - G8	J9 - G9
t-test Sig. (2-tailed)	-	.000	.000	.024	.407	-	-	.000	.003
Exact Sig. (2-tailed)	.004	.004	.004	.039	.426	.004	.004	.004	.004
Dominating Ranks	Java	Java	Java	Java	-	Java	Java	Java	Java

Table 6-21: Results of the t-test and Wilcoxon test for the Groovy starter outperformer group

Both tests confirm that there is a significant difference between the two parts for the outperformer Groovy starters except for task 5. It can be assumed that the outperformers of this group benefitted from a learning effect as well as the language effect of Java that made solving the tasks easier. The non-significant result of task 5 is not a danger to this assumption because it was assumed that there is no difference between the languages for the semantic errors tasks anyway. On to the descriptive statistics of the Groovy starter underperformers:

Task	G1	G2	G3	G4	G5	G6	G7	G8	G9
Median	1033	632	1117	1261	649	1277	895	1184	767
Mean	1086	715	1238	1384	801	1225	907	1240	793
Min.	476	430	799	337	174	633	280	780	246
Max.	2215	1273	2146	3062	2262	1894	1492	1838	1712
Std. Dev.	553	292	478	912	643	383	345	337	504

Table 6-22: Descriptive statistics of Groovy tasks for underperformer participants that started with Groovy (in seconds)

Task	J1	J2	J3	J4	J5	J6	J7	J8	J9
Median	352	500	661	810	196	697	223	598	102
Mean	387	554	704	980	271	709	223	633	139
Min.	233	275	425	324	121	432	78	374	70
Max.	621	1169	1163	2562	637	1039	374	1064	430
Std. Dev.	132	299	234	714	177	194	93	220	119

Table 6-23: Descriptive statistics of Java tasks for underperformer participants that started with Groovy (in seconds)

	Median	Mean	Minimum	Maximum	Standard Derivation
Total Time	14245	13987	10191	16905	2304

Table 6-24: Descriptive statistics of total time for underperformer participants that started with Groovy (in seconds)

Besides the fact that their general values are obviously worse than those of the outperformer group, the underperformer group seems to also have a higher standard derivation (even considerably higher for the total times). It looks as if the group of the underperformers has therefore a largely higher variance in the results. According to the tests for normal distribution, the t-test can be applied to all tasks except task 8. The results of the significance tests show that the times for the tasks between the Java and Groovy part are significantly different for the Underperformer group except for tasks 4 and 5 (the tests display contradicting results for test 5, so conservatively, significance is not assumed).

	J1 - G1	J2 - G2	J3 - G3	J4 - G4	J5 - G5	J6 - G6	J7 - G7	J8 - G8	J9 - G9
t-test Sig. (2-tailed)	.005	.038	.026	.272	.074	.008	.001	-	.009
Exact Sig. (2-tailed)	.008	.039	.039	.250	.039	.016	.008	.008	.008
Dominating Ranks	Java	Java	Java	-	Java	Java	Java	Java	Java

Table 6-25: Results of the t-test and Wilcoxon test for the Groovy starter underperformer group

Concluding, same as the outperformers, the underperformer participants that started with Groovy seem to have benefitted from both the learning effect and the positive effect of the type system. The non-significant results for tasks 4 and 5 are again a hint towards strengthening the assumption that there is no significant difference between the languages for these tasks, although these results seem to oppose the results gained for the whole groups where there was a significant difference even for the semantic error tasks (possibly due to an undesired learning effect).

6.2.4.2 Participants that started with Java

The next step is the analysis of the participant group that started with Java according to the same criteria of out- and underperformers. First the descriptive statistics of the outperformers: It turns out that the best participants that started with Java have larger spreads in their values than the corresponding participants that started with Groovy. This seems true for both parts as well as for the total time.

Task	G1	G2	G3	G4	G5	G6	G7	G8	G9
Median	435	464	1074	239	137	810	750	1009	474
Mean	582	574	1239	334	155	974	883	1010	621
Min.	252	295	591	153	87	549	170	703	315
Max.	1620	1354	2433	719	261	1851	1585	1326	1371
Std. Dev.	444	348	573	197	65	438	500	208	363

Table 6-26: Descriptive statistics of Groovy tasks for outperformer participants that started with Java (in seconds)

Task	J1	J2	J3	J4	J5	J6	J7	J8	J9
Median	522	797	919	1281	323	751	199	736	159
Mean	592	867	875	1157	720	1081	242	724	198
Min.	375	315	649	312	177	626	102	566	102
Max.	914	1590	1069	1822	2264	3240	563	825	535
Std. Dev.	179	467	137	548	809	886	142	89	142

Table 6-27: Descriptive statistics of Java tasks for outperformer participants that started with Java (in seconds)

	Median	Mean	Minimum	Maximum	Standard Derivation
Total Time	13052	12827	9663	15423	2154

Table 6-28: Descriptive statistics of total time for outperformer participants that started with Java (in seconds)

Second, the tests for normal distribution permit the use of the t-test for tasks 2, 3, 4, 6, 7, 8 and 9. The results are shown below. Both tests come to the same conclusions. The results are significantly different for tasks 2, 4, 5, 7, 8 and 9. It is interesting that here the results for the semantic error tasks are actually different, indicating a learning effect again, because they solve them significantly faster using Groovy the second time (at least the assumedly better developers).

	J1 - G1	J2 - G2	J3 - G3	J4 - G4	J5 - G5	J6 - G6	J7 - G7	J8 - G8	J9 - G9
t-test. Sig. (2-tailed)	-	.035	.085	.006	-	.737	.006	.015	.018
Exact Sig. (2-tailed)	.742	.039	.055	.023	.016	.742	.008	.008	.016
Dominating Ranks	-	Groovy	-	Groovy	Groovy	-	Java	Java	Java

Table 6-29: Results of the t-test and Wilcoxon test for the Java starter outperformer group

A surprising result is the one of task 2. A significant difference could be detected which was in favor of Groovy. A possible explanation might be that after task 1 (where there was no significant difference) the better developers caught on to using Groovy quickly and therefore the negative effect of the dynamic type system was compensated for by the developers. This is of course only a speculative explanation, but a likely one because the effect was only true for the second task and the other tasks display the results as expected, no significant difference or a significant difference in favor of Java.

Last group to be analyzed are the Java starter underperformers, again starting with the descriptive statistics.

Task	G1	G2	G3	G4	G5	G6	G7	G8	G9
Median	871	899	1415	662,5	305,5	1016	1289	1271	883
Mean	1043	877,5	1357	849,1	468,6	1151	1335	1444	1208
Min.	227	386	723	222	167	600	665	758	437
Max.	2179	1308	2169	2648	1045	2505	2565	2538	2285
Std. Dev.	722,2	353,2	452,7	774,1	335,1	607	657	585	750

Table 6-30: Descriptive statistics of Groovy tasks for underperformer participants that started with Java (in seconds)

Task	J1	J2	J3	J4	J5	J6	J7	J8	J9
Median	957	1080	1220	2083	906	1104	334	895,5	130
Mean	933	1523	1265	2071	868,9	1130	363,9	951,1	139
Min.	479	613	574	1384	268	582	175	722	98
Max.	1609	4285	1983	2910	1458	1665	900	1514	244
Std. Dev.	370	1208	517	458,4	398,4	353	227,3	259,3	47,7

Table 6-31: Descriptive statistics of Java tasks for underperformer participants that started with Java (in seconds)

	Median	Mean	Minimum	Maximum	Standard Derivation
Total Time	17080	18977	15980	28971	4386

Table 6-32: Descriptive statistics of total time for underperformer participants that started with Java (in seconds)

The underperformer group of the Java starters displays a huge standard derivation for the tasks as well as in total time. Comparing these values to the Groovy starters, it seems that the underperformers in both parts have much higher variance in their values, even if the Java underperformers seem to have the highest. Distributions of the tasks 1, 3, 5, 6, 7, 8 and 9 permit the t-test use.

	J1 - G1	J2 - G2	J3 - G3	J4 - G4	J5 - G5	J6 - G6	J7 - G7	J8 - G8	J9 - G9
t-test Sig. (2-tailed)	.538	-	.767	-	.063	.937	.011	.053	.004
Exact Sig. (2-tailed)	.742	.195	.742	.016	.055	.742	.016	.078	.008
Dominating Ranks	-	-	-	Groovy	-	-	Java	-	Java

Table 6-33: Results of the t-test and Wilcoxon test for the Java starter underperformer group

The results for the underperformers are quite similar as those for the outperformers, except that here task 2 displays results as expected with no significance. Tasks 4 scores are significantly different in favor of Groovy, but task 5 scores are not. It seems that the learning effect that leads to the semantic error tasks getting solved very quickly the second time was also apparent for the Java starters. This is an interesting observation, although no explanation can be offered. Maybe it was a design flaw in the experiment which somehow permitted the better Java starters to notice the similar structures of the tasks between the two parts much easier.

All in all, except a few small exceptions (tasks 4 and 5 being the most prominent), the performance group analysis results are as expected from the hypotheses.

6.2.5 Hypotheses and Task based Analysis

The previous analyses were all mostly targeted on getting a rough overview of the results and to get to know the data. This part splits the tasks by their categories and does some additional evaluation. As a reminder, the hypotheses implied that participants solve tasks with an undocumented API generally faster using a static type system (hypothesis 1), that a greater distance between bug and runtime error occurrence would lead to longer fixing time (2-1) and that the fixing time for semantic errors was similar for dynamic and static type systems (2-2).

6.2.5.1 Tasks 1, 2, 3, 6 and 8

The main hypothesis 1 was already considered in the many analyses above and its results have already been presented in many way. However, another interesting question is how much the number of types to identify influences the time taken. There was no explicit hypothesis for this question, but an analysis might still be interesting. For this reason, a regression analysis on the complete results for both languages was performed.

This means that the data of both groups are included because the most interesting factor here is whether the number of types influences the time taken to solve the tasks and if this time differs between the two used languages. Including both groups' times should also be unproblematic because the learning effect for the type identification tasks could only develop to some degree. The reason is that if participants might have learned to perform faster with the IDE or knew what to expect from this type of task, the main search effort contained in the task was still there and largely unaffected by any learning effects.

From the two diagrams in Figure 6-5 and Figure 6-6 it becomes clear that there is a small effect of the number of types to identify on the time taken. It turns out that this effect is much stronger for Groovy, as the slope of the regression line is a little steeper and R^2 is at 7.1%, while for Java it is only 0.5%. This indicates that type identification gets much more cumbersome much quicker when using a dynamically typed language.

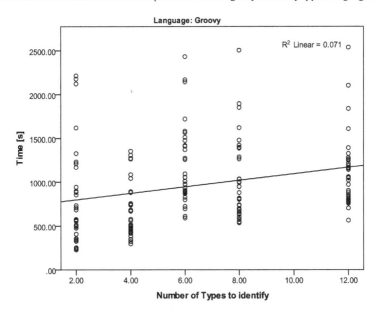

Figure 6-5: Scatterplot of the results for the type identification tasks in Groovy

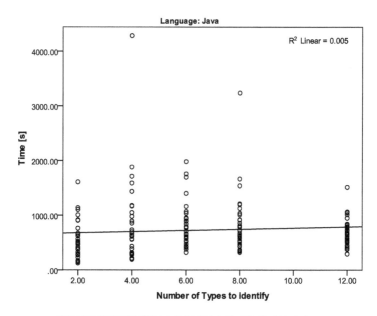

To see how much the combined effect of the language and the number of types had on the time taken to solve the tasks, the regression analysis was configured with the time for the tasks as dependent variable and the language and number of types as independent variables. The results are shown below.

Model	R	R-Square	Adjusted R-Square	Std. Error of the Estimate
1	,282[a]	,079	,074	487,21448

a. Predictors : (Constant), Language, Types

Table 6-34: Results of regression analysis for task time depending on number of types to identify and language

Coefficients[a]					
Model		Unstandardized Coefficients		Standardized Coefficients		
		B	Std. Error	Beta	T	Sig.
1	(Constant)	1040,897	98,396		10,579	,000
	Types	23,898	7,794	,163	3,066	,002
	Language	-232,285	53,641	-,230	-4,330	,000

a. Dependent Variable: Time

Table 6-35: Coefficients of regression analysis for type identification task time depending on number of types to identify and language

The results show that the two variables have a significant impact on the time needed to fulfill a task. It might not strike as very surprising, but it is important to know that these values are significant and this means that the two variables of type number and language are useful predictors for the time it takes to solve a task.

6.2.5.2 Hypothesis 2-1 and Tasks 7 and 9

For hypothesis 2-1 only the Groovy part was interesting, because in Java the errors were merely compile time errors solved quickly. It was therefore not surprising that in all of the above tests the Java parts of tasks 7 and 9 were always found to be solved significantly faster. But the additional hypothesis 2-1 presumes that the farther the place of the bug is removed from the place in the code where it actually leads to a program error, the longer it takes for a programmer to fix it. Thus, the next analysis focuses on the results for tasks 7 and 9 of the Groovy part, which differed.

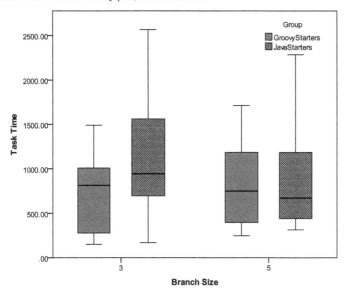

Figure 6-7: Boxplot of the Groovy part results for tasks 7 and 9

In Figure 6-7 the results of the two groups are shown again for tasks 7 and 9. For both groups, the results are rather awkward. It seems that the task 9 was in the majority of cases solved a bit faster, even if the distance between bug and error was a branch size of 5 instead of 3. The results are much more apparent in the Java starters group. It needs to be tested whether this is a significant effect, hence the dependent t-test (the differences of the task are normally-distributed for both groups, exact test results are omitted) and Wilcoxon-test are used.

	GS G7 - GS G9	JS G7 – JS G9
t-test Sig. (2-tailed)	.845	.332
Wilcoxon Exact Sig. (2-tailed)	.927	.323

Table 6-36: Results of t-test and Wilcoxon test for comparing tasks 7 and 9 for Groovy

As can be read from Table 6-36, the times of tasks 7 and 9 are not significantly different from each other for both groups. In the light of these results, a regression analysis would not make any sense and is therefore omitted. It can only be speculated as to why these specific scores were achieved. A simple explanation similar to the one of the semantic error tasks is probably not sufficient and would only apply to the Java starter group anyway. Another explanation could be that task 9 was somehow easier to solve because of its design, even if care was taken to make it the more difficult task. Some factors in its design might have lead to some of the participants needing more time for task 7 instead of 9. Or, the difference of a branch size of 3 versus 5 was simply not big enough to show significant differences. In the end, no new insight could be gained about Hypothesis 2-1.

6.2.5.3 Hypothesis 2-2 and Tasks 4 and 5

As was already said, hypothesis 2-2 was that the fixing of semantic errors would take roughly the same time no matter which type system the language uses. The tasks included for the hypothesis are tasks 4 and 5, the semantic error tasks. The other analyses gave a rather mixed impression for hypothesis 2-2: The general analysis of the overall results and the analysis for residual effects did not detect a significant difference between the two parts for tasks 4 and 5, but the within-subject analysis did.[1] Also, the exploratory analysis based on the different performance groups found mixed results, too. For some performance groups one task showed a significant difference, for some both did. All these inconclusive data lead to the possible explanation that there was a definite learning effect that participants had for these two tasks. The impression from the experiment observation and some video footage confirm that during their second part, the participants were very quick in understanding the problem and finding the solution. So

---

[1] As an addition, the problematic analysis in the appendix found significant differences for task 4, but not for task 5.

it is applicable to assume that they recognized the problem description or code structure. After all, both programs had essentially an identically structure but had their respective domains strapped over them.

As a measure of last resort, there is one possible analysis of the data left that could still produce meaningful results: Comparing only the first try of tasks 4 and 5 of all participants with each other. This means for the Groovy starters, only the Groovy times, and for Java starters, only the Java times of tasks 4 and 5 are part of the analysis and the two groups have to be treated as if they were taken from an independent-measures design. This is because now there is no within-subject data available.

Figure 6-8 shows the data in a box plot form. It can be seen that the difference is not very big for task 5 but is much larger for task 4.

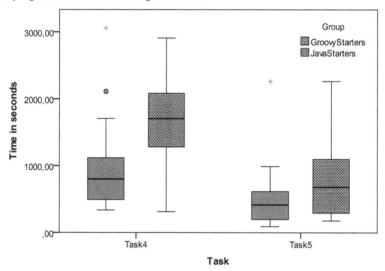

Figure 6-8: Boxplot of results for task 4 and 5 results of only the first language used

The tests for normal distribution yielded no useful results (test scores in the appendix under A.2.3), therefore only the Mann-Whitney-U and Kolmogorov-Smirnov test are applied. Sadly, the two tests for significance do not offer the reason for any new conclusions.

	Task4	Task5
MW-U Exact Sig. (2-tailed)	.015	.217
KS-Z Exact Sig. (2-tailed)	.005	.148
Dominating Ranks	Groovy	-

Table 6-37: Results of Mann-Whitney-U and Kolmogorov-Smirnov-Z test for first tasks 4 and 5 results

If one would only take these results as a base, then hypothesis 2-2 would have to be rejected because task 4 displays results that would falsify it. Careful though should be the consideration of this, as the whole experiment results and the additional data point towards a strong learning effect especially for those two tasks with their special structure. Still, for this experiment, hypothesis 2-2 must be considered as rejected, but no conclusion about its general truth could be drawn from the experiment.

7. Summary and Discussion

In this section, some final remarks are given and the experiment results are summarized and discussed.

7.1 Final Remarks

In the chapter about the experiment's design, it was mentioned that a problematic experiment design would be to use an independent-measures approach. In Appendix A.3, this experiment was treated and analyzed as if it had been an independent-measures design. To increase awareness of this problem in experiment design, the results of this "fictive analysis" will be picked up here. And its results are very different from those of the actual real experiment that was conducted and thoroughly analyzed. Without going into too much detail here (the results are in the appendix), it turned out that an independent-measures design would have led to very different results: Because in the independent design experiment almost no significant difference between the two type systems was measured, except for one task whose results were in favor of the dynamic type system. There are many possible consequences if this fictive design had been the real design: It would have led to a rejection of the main hypothesis and completely different conclusions. In the best case, the results are correct and could be confirmed in further similar experiments. But as is the case in this example, the results are different. This could have many implications, assuming this work would stay one of the few experiments on the topic. One result could be that other researches take the results for granted and quote them in their works. Even worse, additional research and theories could possibly have been created based on experiment results that are at least problematic when it comes to validity, if not fundamentally wrong.

7.2 Result Summary

The within-subject analysis of the complete data yielded positive results. A significant difference in favor of Java for the type identification tasks (except for task 2 where it is not significant), no significant difference for tasks 4 and 5 (the semantic error tasks) and a significant difference in favor of Java for tasks 7 and 9 (the latent type errors). However, the complete data results are problematic because a strong residual/sequence effect was believed to be contained in the data.

Therefore, as a next step, an attempt was made to test if the sequence effect between the groups (Java first or Groovy first) had a significant impact. For this, the Java and Groovy part results were tested for significant differences. The results were that there is a very significant impact of the starting language on the Java tasks and on some of the Groovy tasks. Consequently, a residual (or carry-over) effect of the starting language was assumed and the two groups were analyzed separately. It is not clear if this approach is the methodically correct one to calculate or identify carry-over or residual effects, but it was chosen because there is no methodology for this problem in software engineering experimentation available and it seems a reasonable thing to do.

After continuing the analysis for the groups separately, the within-subject analysis of the Groovy starter group revealed that there was a significant difference in task times between the two parts for all tasks, meaning that participants where significantly faster using the Java (their second) part; a finding that supports the main hypothesis. The effect that was assumed and presented in Figure 4-1 seems to have manifested itself in the predicted way. The results for the Java starter group were not as clear but still encouraging. Except for task 2 (where for some reason the significance was in favor of Groovy), all other tasks displayed the expected results: No significant difference or a significant difference in favor of Java for the larger type identification tasks. Task 4 and 5 results seemed to be biased by a learning effect for both results, as the second time was always the part solved quicker. The tasks 7 and 9 display the expected picture of Java outperforming over Groovy in both cases. All these results speak strongly in favor of the static type system and it can be concluded that for an undocumented API this effect is genuine.

Next was the exploratory approach of splitting the two participant groups each into two new halves of out- and underperformers and applying the within-subject analyses on these four groups. For the Groovy starter out- and underperformers, almost all tasks displayed significant difference between task times except for task 5 (no significance in the outperformer group) and task 4 (no significance in the underperformer group). This is a slight difference from the results of the complete Groovy starter group, and the two scores (out and underperformers together) combined probably lead to the significant results for the complete group data. The Java starter outperformer scores were very similar to those of their complete group analysis data and tasks 4 and 5 both yielded significantly different times. The underperformer Java starters produced different results, with no significant differences for all type identification tasks and only significantly different results for task 4. This is not surprising and still satisfactory, because positive learning effect and negative language effect seemed to have canceled each other out for the Java underperformers. For all four groups, Tasks 7 and 9 always displayed the same expected results already mentioned above.

Last was the additional analysis of the task type results. For the type identification tasks, a small but significant prediction effect of the number of types to identify on the taken time could be seen using a regression analysis. The same could not be said for the latent type error tasks, where there was no significant difference between the results for a stack branch of 3 and 5 at all. Finally, the tasks 4 and 5 analysis based on only the first of each participant for the two tasks could not provide a useful insight, as task 4 times differed significantly while task 5 times did not.

The impact on the hypotheses can be summarized as follows: The main hypothesis 1 holds in light of all analyses results, meaning that a type system seems to speed up the solving of tasks using an undocumented API. The hypotheses 2-1 and 2-2 would need to be rejected based on the gained data and their alternative hypothesis has to be assumed. Of course, there are reasonable doubts about the results for the last two hypotheses because of some learning effects that are assumed to have occurred.

7.3 Discussion

The results of the experiment are encouraging. It can be assumed that the positive effect of the static type system is a genuine one, and also that the more types a developer has to identify, the longer it takes him to finish a task.

But it is reasonable to discuss the experiment design itself and some of the approaches used. First, there are alternatives to a repeated-measures design in terms of control over systematic/unsystematic variation. One is blocking (grouping) of participants into similar groups. This means if the experiment conductor would know that six participants are good developers and another six are average developers, he would equally distribute them into the two groups, ending up with three good and average developers in each group. This would remove a huge amount of unsystematic variation, because their development skill is very likely to be a major factor. The problem here is that there is no scientifically valid and reliable method that can be used to objectively measure someone's development skills. Some experiments use questionnaires and self-estimation of the participants to discover their development skills. But as was examined in one of this authors' own works [Kleinschmager and Hanenberg 2011], this approach cannot really produce reliable results (Hanenberg also criticizes this rather liberal use of questionnaires and the general lack of experimentation knowledge in software engineering [Hanenberg 2010c]). Another method in experiments from other sciences is to use control groups which serve as a kind of "null" group for comparison where any effect is completely absent, as no manipulation is done on them (in medicine often via administering placebos). This is an approach that does not really apply to this kind of experiment, as there is no comparable language that has neither a static nor a dynamic type system.

As to the learning effect that was discovered, it is one of the hardest tasks in software engineering experiment design to produce applications and tasks that can be compared without too much variance between them. They need to have similar structure and complexity and in the best case be still so different that participants would not benefit from solving either of them first. In this experiment, the approach of application migration was used. This was done by first designing the application for one part of the experiment and then taking it and completely renaming all code artifacts to create a different domain. However -as a personal side note on some observation during the experiment- it turned out that this approach could have been insufficient (even with the additional obfuscation techniques applied), because from an experimenters point of view it seemed that participants recognized the similar structure of the two applications. This was no big problem for the type identification tasks because they included a search and code writing effort anyway, but was especially harmful for the error finding task types. For future experiments, different approaches might have to be found.

In addition, one could argue that the usage of a totally undocumented API where even the variable names do not exactly represent their contained types is quite unfair towards the dynamic type system. A reasonable next step would therefore be a very similar experiment (possibly even a modified repetition of this one) with variable names that reflect their contained types. In addition, possible work ahead could be more exploratory data mining on the experiment data concerning the influence of the personality types on the results and also the impact of other data that have been gathered (e.g. how many times a participant used the search function of the IDE).

8. Conclusion

For this thesis, a controlled experiment on the impact of static and dynamic type systems on development time was conducted. The motivation for this work was the generally scarce amount of experiments in software engineering and the fact that often the advantages and disadvantages of type systems are discussed but seldom tried to evaluate empirically. Especially the documentational value of a type system is regularly brought forward along with its ability to find routine programming errors during compile time. Software maintenance (which includes extending and debugging software) is generally believed to make up a big part of the general costs of software projects and therefore development time needed in this part of the software life cycle could be reduced if there were a positive impact of type systems. This becomes even more important when keeping in mind that in many cases the code of the software is the only available or only up-to-date source of information on a program.

So the main hypothesis of the experiment was that a static type system has a positive impact on the time needed to fulfill tasks with an undocumented API. Two additional hypotheses were also part of the experiment. One stated that for fixing semantic errors there is no difference in time taken no matter which type system is used, and the second one stated that when searching runtime errors with a dynamic type system, the farther away a bug is from the location where it results in an error, the longer it takes to fix the bug.

The 36 participants that took part in the experiment had to solve several tasks in Java as well as in Groovy and for this had been split into two groups. One group started with Java and one with Groovy and they then had to solve the corresponding second part afterwards. There were three categories of tasks. The first task category needed the participants to identify and use a number of different types in the workspace. Five tasks belonged to this category. The second category was made up of two tasks that contained a semantic error that needed fixing. Finally, the two tasks in the third category included a "latent type error", where the actual bug location was different from the point where the bug resulted in program termination. These last tasks were type errors that lead to a compile time error in Java but a runtime error in Groovy, making them much harder to find in Groovy.

In the end, usable data was gathered from 33 participants that solved tall tasks in both languages. The results discovered for the main hypothesis are encouraging: They indicate that there is a significant positive impact of a type system when solving programming tasks with an undocumented API. Consequently, the main hypothesis was hardened, especially when considering that some previous experiments have led to similar results. The two other hypotheses had to be rejected because of contradicting and insignificant results, but their results very probably suffered from a learning effect in the experiment. Nevertheless, because of the positive results for the main hypothesis, the experiment can be counted as a success. A possible next step would be a repetition to increase external validity and reliability of the results or a variation of the experiment using a documented API and comparing its results to the results from this experiment.

This experiment's results pose a good start on discovering differences on programmer performance between static and dynamic type systems, especially because there a very few studies at all, but more studies are needed to confirm them.

References

APACHE FOUNDATION. *Apache Ant Homepage.* http://ant.apache.org/. Accessed 7 October 2011.

BASILI, V., AND SELBY, R. 1991. Paradigms for Experimentation and Empirical Studies in Software Engineering. *Reliability Engineering and System Safety vol. 32*, 1-2, 171–193.

BASILI, V.R. 1996. The role of experimentation in software engineering: past, current, and future. In *Proceedings of the 18th international conference on Software engineering*. IEEE Computer Society, Washington, DC, USA, 442-449.

BOEHM, B.W. 1976. Software Engineering. *IEEE Transactions on Computers 25*, 1226–1241.

BORTZ, J., AND DÖRING, N. 2006. *Forschungsmethoden und Evaluation für Human- und Sozialwissenschaftler. Mit 87 Tabellen.* Springer-Lehrbuch. Springer, Heidelberg.

BRACHA, G. 2004. Pluggable type systems. In *OOPSLA '04 Workshop on Revival of Dynamic Languages.*

BROY, M., DEISSENBOECK, F., AND PIZKA, M. 2006. Demystifying maintainability. In *Proceedings of the 2006 international workshop on Software quality*. ACM, New York, NY, USA, 21-26.

BUSS, E., AND HENSHAW, J. 1992. Experiences in program understanding. In *Proceedings of the 1992 conference of the Centre for Advanced Studies on Collaborative research - Volume 1*. IBM Press, 157-189.

CARDELLI, L. 1997. Type Systems. In *The Computer Science and Engineering Handbook*, ALLEN B. TUCKER, Ed. CRC Press, 2208–2236.

CARDELLI, L., AND WEGNER, P. 1985. On understanding types, data abstraction, and polymorphism. *ACM Comput. Surv 17*, 471-523. http://doi.acm.org/10.1145/6041.6042 Pick It! ,

CARVER, J., JACCHERI, L., MORASCA, S., AND SHULL, F. 2003. Issues in Using Students in Empirical Studies in Software Engineering Education. In *Proceedings of the 9th International Symposium on Software Metrics*. IEEE Computer Society, Washington, DC, USA, 239-.

CODEHAUS. *Groovy Homepage.* http://groovy.codehaus.org/. Accessed 7 October 2011.

COSTA, P.&.M.R. 1992. *Revised NEO Personality Inventory (NEO PI-R) and NEO Five Factor Inventory (NEO-FFI). Professional manual.* Psychological Assessment Resources, Odessa, Fl.

DALY, M., SAZAWAL, V., AND FOSTER J. 2009. Work in Progress: an Empirical Study of Static Typing in Ruby. *Workshop on Evaluation and Usability of Programming Languages and Tools (PLATEAU) at ON-WARD 2009.*

DAS, S., LUTTERS, W.G., AND SEAMAN, C.B. 2007. Understanding documentation value in software maintenance. In *CHIMIT '07: Proceedings of the 2007 symposium on Computer human interaction for the management of information technology.* ACM Press, New York, NY, USA.

DELOREY, D.P., KNUTSON, C.D., AND CHUN, S. 2007. Do Programming Languages Affect Productivity? A Case Study Using Data from Open Source Projects. *Emerging Trends in FLOSS Research and Development, International Workshop on 0*, 8.

DENNING, P.J. 2005. Is Computer Science Science? *Communications of the ACM 48*, 4, 27–31.

DUCASSÉ, M., AND EMDE, A.-M. 1988. A review of automated debugging systems: knowledge, strategies and techniques. In *Proceedings of the 10th international conference on Software engineering.* IEEE Computer Society Press, Los Alamitos, CA, USA, 162-171.

FIELD, A. 2009. *Discovering Statistics Using SPSS (Introducing Statistical Methods).* Sage Publications Ltd.

FURR, M., AN, J.-H., FOSTER, J.S., AND HICKS, M. 2009. Static type inference for Ruby. In *Proceedings of the 2009 ACM symposium on Applied Computing.* ACM, New York, NY, USA, 1859-1866.

GANNON, J.D. 1977. An experimental evaluation of data type conventions. *Commun. ACM 20*, 584-595.

GAT, E. 2000. Lisp as an Alternative to Java. *Intelligence 11.* http://www.flownet.com/gat/papers/lisp-java.pdf.

GÉNOVA, G. 2010. Is computer science truly scientific? *Commun. ACM 53*, 7, 37–39.

GOSLING, J., AND MCGILTON, H. 1996. *The Java Language Environment.* Sun Microsystems.

GOULD, J. 1975. Some psychological evidence on how people debug computer programs. *International Journal of Man-Machine Studies 7*, 2, 151-182.

HALL, P.A.V. 1992. Overview of reverse engineering and reuse research. *Inf. Softw. Technol 34*, 239-249. http://dl.acm.org/citation.cfm?id=150362.150366.

HANENBERG, S. 2010a. An experiment about static and dynamic type systems: doubts about the positive impact of static type systems on development time. *SIGPLAN Not 45*, 22-35.

HANENBERG, S. 2010b. Doubts about the positive impact of static type systems on programming tasks in single developer projects - an empirical study. In *Proceedings of the 24th European conference on Object-oriented programming.* Springer-Verlag, Berlin, Heidelberg, 300-303.

HANENBERG, S. 2010c. Faith, hope, and love. In *Proceedings of the ACM international conference on Object oriented programming systems languages and applications - OOPSLA '10.* ACM Press, 933.

HANENBERG, S. 2011. A Chronological Experience Report from an Initial Experiment Series on Static Type Systems. *Workshop on Empirical Evaluation of Programming Language Constructs.*

HENNING, M. 2007. API Design Matters. *Queue 5,* 24-36.

HÖST, M., REGNELL, B., AND WOHLIN, C. 2000. Using Students as Subjects - A Comparative Study ofStudents and Professionals in Lead-Time Impact Assessment. *Empirical Softw. Engg 5,* 201-214. http://dl.acm.org/citation.cfm?id=594537.594544.

HUDAK, P., AND JONES, M.P. 1994. *Haskell vs. Ada Vs. C++ vs Awk vs ... An Experiment in Software Prototyping Productivity.*

IEEE. 1998. *1219-1998 IEEE Standard for Software Maintenance.*

ISO/IEC/IEEE. 2006. *ISO/IEC 14764 IEEE Std 14764-2006.*

JONES, B., AND KENWARD, M.G. 1989. *Design and analysis of cross-over trials.* Monographs on statistics and applied probability 34. Chapman and Hall, London [u.a.].

JUNIT, *JUnit Homepage.* http://www.junit.org/. Accessed 7 October 2011.

JURISTO, N., AND MORENO, A.M. 2001. *Basics of software engineering experimentation.* Kluwer Academic Publishers, Boston, Mass. [u.a.].

KATZ, I., AND ANDERSON, J. 1987. Debugging: An Analysis of Bug-Location Strategies. *Human-Comp. Interaction 3,* 4, 351–399.

KLEINSCHMAGER, S. 2009. *A Controlled Experiment for Measuring the Impact of Aspect-Oriented Programming on Software Development Time.* Bachelor Thesis, University of Duisburg-Essen.

KLEINSCHMAGER, S., AND HANENBERG, S. 2011. How to rate programming skills in programming experiments? A preliminary, exploratory study based on university marks, pretests, and self-estimation. *PLATEAU - 4th Evaluation and Usability of Programming Languages and Tools at SPLASH.*

LAMPORT, L., AND PAULSON, L.C. 1999. Should your specification language be typed. *ACM Trans. Program. Lang. Syst 21,* 502-526. http://doi.acm.org/10.1145/319301.319317 Pick It! ,

LIENTZ, B.P., SWANSON, E.B., AND TOMPKINS, G.E. 1978. Characteristics of application software maintenance. *Commun. ACM 21,* 466-471.

LUKOWICZ, P., HEINZ, E.A., PRECHELT, L., AND TICHY, W.F. 1994. Experimental Evaluation in Computer Science: A Quantitative Study. *Journal of Systems and Software 28*, 9-18.

MARTIN, R.C. 2009. *Clean code. A handbook of agile software craftsmanship.* Robert C. Martin series. Prentice Hall, Upper Saddle River, NJ [u.a.].

MAYER, C. 2011. *An empirical study of possible effects of static type systems on documentation - a controlled experiment with an undocumented application programming interface.* Bachelor Thesis, University of Duisburg-Essen.

MURPHY, L., LEWANDOWSKI, G., MCCAULEY, R., SIMON, B., THOMAS, L., AND ZANDER, C. 2008. Debugging: the good, the bad, and the quirky - a qualitative analysis of novices' strategies. *SIGCSE Bull 40*, 163-167.

PIERCE, B.C. 2002. *Types and programming languages.* Ex. mit 13-stelliger und ohne 13-stellige ISBN. MIT Press, Cambridge, Mass. [u.a.].

POPPER, K.R. 2008. *The Logic of scientific discovery.* Routledge classics. Routledge, London.

PRECHELT, L., 2000. *An empirical comparison of C, C++, Java, Perl, Python, Rexx, and Tcl for a search/string-processing program.*

PRECHELT, L. 2001. *Kontrollierte Experimente in der Softwaretechnik. Potenzial und Methodik.* Springer, Berlin [u.a.].

PRECHELT, L., AND TICHY, W.F. 1998. A Controlled Experiment to Assess the Benefits of Procedure Argument Type Checking. *IEEE Transactions on Software Engineering 24*, 302-312.

RUNESON, P. 2003. Using Students as Experiment Subjects – An Analysis on Graduate and Freshmen Student Data. In *Proceedings of the 7th International Conference on Empirical Assessment & Evaluation in Software Engineering*, 95–102.

SCHNEIDEWIND, N.F. 1987. The State of Software Maintenance. *IEEE Trans. Softw. Eng 13*, 303-310. http://dl.acm.org/citation.cfm?id=29740.29741.

SINGER, J., LETHBRIDGE, T., VINSON, N., AND ANQUETIL, N. 1997. An examination of software engineering work practices. In *Proceedings of the 1997 conference of the Centre for Advanced Studies on Collaborative research.* IBM Press, 21-.

SNELTING, G. 1998. Paul Feyerabend and software technology. *International Journal on Software Tools for Technology Transfer 2*, 1, 1-5. http://pp.info.uni-karlsruhe.de/uploads/publikationen/snelting98sttt.pdf.

SNELTING, G. 2001. Feyerabend – zwei Jahre später. *Informatik-Spektrum 24*, 305–308. http://dx.doi.org/10.1007/s002870100182.

SOUSA, M.J. 1998. A Survey on the Software Maintenance Process. In *Proceedings of the International Conference on Software Maintenance.* IEEE Computer Society, Washington, DC, USA, 265-.

SOUZA, S.C.B. DE, ANQUETIL, N., AND OLIVEIRA, K.M. DE. 2005. A study of the documentation essential to software maintenance. In *Proceedings of the 23rd annual international conference on Design of communication: documenting & designing for pervasive information.* ACM, New York, NY, USA, 68-75.

STANDISH, T.A. 1984. An Essay on Software Reuse. *IIEEE Trans. Software Eng SE-10,* 5, 494–497.

STARON, M. 2007. Using Students as Subjects in Experiments-A Quantitative Analysis of the Influence of Experimentation on Students' Learning Proces. In *Proceedings of the 20th Conference on Software Engineering Education & Training.* IEEE Computer Society, Washington, DC, USA, 221-228.

STEINBERG, M. 2011. *What is the impact of static type systems on maintenance tasks? An empirical study of differences in debugging time using statically and dynamically typed languages.* Master Thesis, University of Duisburg-Essen.

STRACHAN, J. 2003. *Groovy - the birth of a new dynamic language for the Java platform.* http://radio-weblogs.com/0112098/2003/08/29.html. Accessed 7 October 2011.

STUCHLIK, A., AND HANENBERG, S. 2011. Static vs. dynamic type systems: An empirical study about the relationship between type casts and development time. *Proceedings of Dynamic Language Symposium.*

TICHY, W.F. 1997. Should Computer Scientists Experiment More? - 16 Excuses to Avoid Experimentation. *IEEE Computer 31,* 32-40.

TJORTJIS, C., AND LAYZELL, P. 2001. Expert Maintainers' Strategies and Needs when Understanding Software: A Qualitative Empirical Study. In *Proceedings of the IEEE 8th Asia-Pacific Software Engineering Conference (APSEC 2001), IEEE Computer.* Press, 281-287.

TRATT, L. 2009. Dynamically Typed Languages. *Advances in Computers 77,* 149–184.

VESSEY, I. 1986. Expertise in debugging computer programs: an analysis of the content of verbal protocols. *IEEE Trans. Syst. Man Cybern 16,* 621-637. http://dl.acm.org/citation.cfm?id=10468.10469.

WOHLIN, C. 2000. *Experimentation in software engineering. An introduction.* The Kluwer international series in software engineering 6. Kluwer, Boston [u.a.].

A. Appendix

A.1 Statistical Methods and Tests

The following statistical methods, diagram types and tests are used in the experiment and will only be explained roughly, omitting any mathematics for the sake of a short overview. For a more thorough explanation, refer to any statistics book, like [Field 2009], which is a very well-written and fun to read book about statistics, experimental research, experiment design and how to use the SPSS statistics application.

A.1.1. Box plots (box-whisker-diagrams)

Boxplots (also called box-whiskey-diagrams) are diagrams that visualize different statistical variables of a certain dataset. Among others, they show the median, the distribution of the lowest and largest quartile and also display their variability. Boxplots can also include the explicit display of outliers and extremes in their representation

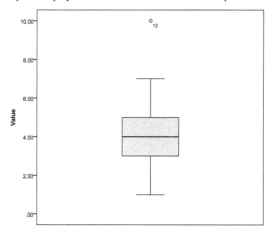

Figure A-1: Example of a box plot

The line in the middle shows the median, the two top and bottom whiskers represent the two top and lower quartiles and the big boxes represent the middle 50%. Outliers are shown explicitly in the boxplot as dots with their corresponding line number in the dataset. If they are strong outliers they can be displayed as asterisks (they are then sometimes called extremes).

A.1.2. Kolmogorov-Smirnov and Shapiro-Wilk

The Kolmogorov-Smirnov (K-S) and Shapiro-Wilk (S-W) tests are used to check whether a given sample can be assumed to be normally-distributed. The way they do it is that they compare the values of the sample to a normally distributed set of values with same mean and standard derivation. The result is compared to a table of z-scores (or critical values) and a p-value. In short words, the p-value can be considered as the probability that the results are a product of random occurrence. A common value for p is 0.05, meaning that it is 95% certain that the result is genuine.

If the resulting p-value is significant ($p < 0.05$) it means, that the sample's distribution does significantly differ from a normal distribution, thus cannot be considered normally distributed. A value greater than 0.05 means that the distribution does not differ significantly and a normal-distribution can be assumed for this sample. In general, the S-W test is said to have a higher power, especially with smaller samples, which is why in this work, in any contradicting situation, the results of the S-W test are given higher precedence.

A.1.3. Independent and Dependent t-test

When there are different experiment conditions and different participants have been used in each of them (called independent-measures design), the independent t-test can be used. It assumes normal distribution in the two sets of data to be compared, and also that the variances in these two populations are about equal (which is also called homogeneity of variance). And it assumes that the two sets are independent and not related. Roughly spoken, it calculates the differences of the means of the sets and compares them according to certain criteria.

The dependent t-test is used if participants were subjected to all of the experiment conditions and therefore functions as a test for within-subject or repeated-measures designs. It works similar to the independent t-test but only assumes a normal distribution. But for the dependent t-test, it is necessary to check whether the differences of the two experiment conditions are normally distributed, not the data themselves.

A.1.4.   Wilcoxon Signed Rank Test

The Wilcoxon Signed Rank test (often just called Wilcoxon test, although there are different Wilcoxon tests, which can lead to confusion) is a non-parametric test that can be used to check for difference in samples without needing the assumption of normal distribution. As an explanation, for this work, it should be sufficient to say that parametric tests depend on distribution catalogues and therefore specific assumption need to be true. This is not the case for non-parametric tests. So, if two related sets of values need to be compared of which one or both are not normally distributed, the Wilcoxon test can be used.

To simplify: The way the test works is that it first orders all results for both samples to be compared, assigns ranks in that order, ties the ranks, and then calculates the tests significance result based on the smaller sum of the two sample ranks.

A.1.5.   Mann-Whitney-U and Kolmogorov-Smirnov Z test

These two tests are non-parametric tests to compare two independent samples, as used in the fictional problematic experiment design analysis in A.3. The Mann-Whitney-U test uses a similar approach as the Wilcoxon-Signed Rank test by ordering, ranking and tying results, although the statistics are calculated differently. The results are interpreted as significant if $p < 0.05$.

A.1.6.   Regression Analysis

Regression Analysis is a way of testing whether one or more independent variables can be used to predict a dependent one. Simplified, it uses the actual input data and tries to construct a fitting model for prediction and also calculates how well this model can predict these values and how much error is still contained in the model. There are some regression types, but the only one used in this work is linear regression, which is also the most common. When trying to explain it graphically, it works by plotting the data into a graph and then drawing a line through the points that is kind of an ideal line predicting the data. This line is called the regression line. The line slope, intercept and gradient are calculated by the regression analysis, providing the user with a kind of ideal model to predict further values from current data.

A.2 Supplemental Data

A.2.1. Participant Results Tasks 1 to 9 (Java)

Number	Task1	Task2	Task3	Task4	Task5	Task6	Task7	Task8	Task9
2	286	432	663	1141	169	812	197	584	70
4	233	567	1163	554	210	675	130	612	106
7	382	308	425	476	121	432	206	565	80
8	124	214	418	181	136	536	100	385	67
12	146	215	414	104	127	323	98	434	46
13	413	301	520	187	76	367	88	514	44
15	522	293	579	489	86	473	172	671	210
18	170	209	468	583	139	576	139	526	127
19	502	313	470	1163	419	858	374	374	94
21	621	1169	846	1015	293	1039	298	1064	108
23	166	313	432	281	74	511	116	450	137
25	288	669	612	2562	637	526	262	664	127
26	153	196	535	220	467	344	129	501	244
27	321	275	793	604	181	610	240	409	430
30	411	286	381	350	673	443	169	543	116
33	271	193	320	626	90	358	137	293	53
35	459	700	659	324	137	719	78	795	97

Table A-1: Participants raw results for the Java part in seconds for Groovy Starters

Number	Task1	Task2	Task3	Task4	Task5	Task6	Task7	Task8	Task9
0	483	315	649	1205	219	791	187	645	114
3	562	981	1038	1930	268	1212	175	1016	98
5	375	388	941	584	240	1127	563	566	108
6	764	558	938	1764	475	3240	286	740	535
9	1139	613	574	2256	337	582	344	735	153
10	479	1178	1983	2910	1022	1197	900	782	244
14	1106	895	893	2166	927	1011	324	841	103
16	914	1051	842	787	325	716	173	732	192
17	673	1590	711	1423	177	650	160	691	102
20	907	1713	773	1642	1458	920	352	722	144
22	1609	4285	1697	2278	1174	1541	200	1514	116
24	1007	1883	1757	2000	880	1665	268	950	146
29	484	735	953	1356	320	626	210	825	215
31	560	858	1069	312	2264	781	258	823	147
32	651	637	1401	1384	885	915	348	1049	105
34	480	1437	899	1822	1740	720	102	772	170

Table A-2: Participants raw results for the Java part in seconds for Java Starters

A.2.2. Participant Results Tasks 1 to 9 (Groovy)

Number	Task1	Task2	Task3	Task4	Task5	Task6	Task7	Task8	Task9
2	1212	463	1258	3062	174	1397	813	1021	332
4	507	892	828	2110	828	950	1009	780	1308
7	886	516	901	492	990	1288	280	1060	783
8	709	345	696	1117	358	685	263	862	926
12	343	578	1010	788	92	537	149	785	273
13	563	483	904	458	420	602	927	770	1571
15	568	418	893	747	170	663	739	797	1263
18	241	452	1371	543	360	1621	258	884	510
19	2215	748	799	984	684	633	1123	1838	812
21	1169	1273	1274	1707	382	1894	747	1608	398
23	408	497	1008	1091	611	808	308	812	413
25	476	516	2146	1537	471	1422	847	1156	1712
26	1232	562	611	407	197	575	1371	564	636
27	897	430	1720	841	2262	1266	1492	1211	750
30	494	742	880	801	127	698	278	844	1186
33	733	682	978	358	416	880	1337	832	277
35	1328	881	976	337	614	948	943	1248	246

Table A-3: Participants raw results for the Groovy part in seconds for Groovy Starters

Number	Task1	Task2	Task3	Task4	Task5	Task6	Task7	Task8	Task9
0	252	322	1055	153	107	803	772	1141	450
3	227	386	2169	222	774	2505	1375	1262	547
5	684	419	2433	197	261	549	1558	1326	315
6	512	295	1093	377	120	1388	550	971	498
9	2179	1265	1411	417	167	1479	1202	1054	437
10	575	439	1054	1042	282	818	665	758	2275
14	943	1042	1566	809	177	997	730	1279	1604
16	1620	508	869	226	140	741	728	798	381
17	358	677	591	252	87	640	170	703	594
20	886	739	1581	330	329	600	732	1391	761
22	2124	756	932	2648	1045	1036	2565	1166	2285
24	556	1308	1419	686	742	1034	1845	2104	1004
29	325	349	1475	218	134	1851	1118	904	1371
31	563	669	1513	719	251	817	582	1189	958
32	856	1085	723	639	233	735	1565	2538	752
34	339	1354	883	531	142	1004	1585	1046	397

Table A-4: Participants raw results for the Groovy part in seconds for Java Starters

A.2.3. Results of the Tests for Normal Distribution on the results split by the two Groups

	Kolmogorov-Smirnov[a]			Shapiro-Wilk		
	Statistics	df	Sig.	Statistics	df	Sig.
GS J1	.142	16	.200*	.936	16	.303
GS J2	.343	16	.000	.680	16	.000
GS J3	.180	16	.174	.848	16	.013
GS J4	.271	16	.003	.758	16	.001
GS J5	.255	16	.007	.793	16	.002
GS J6	.163	16	.200*	.903	16	.091
GS J7	.188	16	.135	.899	16	.078
GS J8	.161	16	.200*	.860	16	.019
GS J9	.279	16	.002	.754	16	.001
JS J1	.168	16	.200*	.889	16	.053
JS J2	.195	16	.107	.738	16	.000
JS J3	.251	16	.008	.860	16	.019
JS J4	.102	16	.200*	.979	16	.952
JS J5	.207	16	.065	.869	16	.027
JS J6	.248	16	.010	.707	16	.000
JS J7	.275	16	.002	.764	16	.001
JS J8	.244	16	.012	.807	16	.003
JS J9	.256	16	.006	.625	16	.000
GS G1	.176	16	.200*	.840	16	.010
GS G2	.225	16	.029	.818	16	.005
GS G3	.257	16	.006	.849	16	.013
GS G4	.222	16	.035	.837	16	.009
GS G5	.235	16	.018	.712	16	.000
GS G6	.195	16	.107	.884	16	.045
GS G7	.211	16	.055	.910	16	.116
GS G8	.250	16	.009	.824	16	.006
GS G9	.133	16	.200*	.923	16	.185
JS G1	.230	16	.024	.797	16	.003
JS G2	.158	16	.200*	.888	16	.051
JS G3	.162	16	.200*	.927	16	.221
JS G4	.235	16	.018	.655	16	.000
JS G5	.292	16	.001	.727	16	.000
JS G6	.270	16	.003	.818	16	.005
JS G7	.209	16	.059	.933	16	.273
JS G8	.241	16	.014	.815	16	.004
JS G9	.219	16	.039	.809	16	.004

a. Lilliefors Significance Correction

*. This is a lower bound of the true significance.

Table A-5: Results of tests for normal distribution on task results split by group (GS = GroovyStarters, JS=JavaStarters)

A.2.4. Results of Tests for Normal Distribution for the Participant Performance Analyses

	Kolmogorov-Smirnov^a			Shapiro-Wilk		
	Statistics	df	Sig.	Statistics	df	Sig.
Task1 Diff	.263	9	.074	.810	9	.027
Task2 Diff	.204	9	.200*	.897	9	.232
Task3 Diff	.116	9	.200*	.987	9	.991
Task4 Diff	.150	9	.200*	.970	9	.897
Task5 Diff	.198	9	.200*	.939	9	.573
Task6 Diff	.350	9	.002	.672	9	.001
Task7 Diff	.292	9	.026	.818	9	.033
Task8 Diff	.156	9	.200*	.957	9	.769
Task9 Diff	.276	9	.047	.860	9	.096

a. Lilliefors Significance Correction

*. This is a lower bound of the true significance.

Table A-6: Tests for Normal Distribution on Differences between Groovy and Java times for Groovy Starter Outperformers

	Kolmogorov-Smirnov^a			Shapiro-Wilk		
	Statistics	df	Sig.	Statistics	df	Sig.
Task1 Diff	.226	8	.200*	.877	8	.177
Task2 Diff	.146	8	.200*	.982	8	.974
Task3 Diff	.218	8	.200*	.935	8	.560
Task4 Diff	.194	8	.200*	.944	8	.651
Task5 Diff	.201	8	.200*	.849	8	.093
Task6 Diff	.195	8	.200*	.886	8	.215
Task7 Diff	.161	8	.200*	.976	8	.943
Task8 Diff	.315	8	.019	.800	8	.029
Task9 Diff	.243	8	.181	.873	8	.162

a. Lilliefors Significance Correction

*. This is a lower bound of the true significance.

Table A-7: Tests for Normal Distribution on Differences between Groovy and Java times for Groovy Starter Underperformers

	Kolmogorov-Smirnov^a			Shapiro-Wilk		
	Statistics	df	Sig.	Statistics	df	Sig.
Task1 Diff	.271	8	.086	.820	8	.047
Task2 Diff	.162	8	.200*	.911	8	.365
Task3 Diff	.254	8	.138	.825	8	.053
Task4 Diff	.272	8	.083	.852	8	.100
Task5 Diff	.356	8	.004	.717	8	.004
Task6 Diff	.295	8	.039	.874	8	.165
Task7 Diff	.172	8	.200*	.966	8	.866
Task8 Diff	.169	8	.200*	.925	8	.470
Task9 Diff	.213	8	.200*	.903	8	.309

a. Lilliefors Significance Correction

*. This is a lower bound of the true significance.

Table A-8: Tests for Normal Distribution on Differences between Groovy and Java times for Java Starter Outperformers

	Kolmogorov-Smirnov[a]			Shapiro-Wilk		
	Statistics	df	Sig.	Statistics	df	Sig.
Task1 Diff	.173	8	.200*	.939	8	.603
Task2 Diff	.276	8	.074	.823	8	.050
Task3 Diff	.253	8	.140	.851	8	.097
Task4 Diff	.299	8	.034	.820	8	.046
Task5 Diff	.188	8	.200*	.940	8	.612
Task6 Diff	.270	8	.090	.828	8	.057
Task7 Diff	.133	8	.200*	.979	8	.960
Task8 Diff	.161	8	.200*	.968	8	.885
Task9 Diff	.239	8	.200*	.871	8	.156

a. Lilliefors Significance Correction
*. This is a lower bound of the true significance.

Table A-9: Tests for Normal Distribution on Differences between Groovy and Java times for Java Starter Underperformers

A.2.5. Participant Performance Analysis based on the complete data

This chapter contains the data for the analysis of the two participant out- and underperformer groups, but not inside the two groups and done on the complete data. Splitting the complete data lead to two groups, with 17 participants in the outperformer and 16 in the underperformer group. The descriptive statistics, tests for normal distribution and significance tests of both groups are shown in this chapter as supplemental data.

A.2.5.1. Outperformers

First the descriptive statistics for the outperformers of the overall experiment data:

Task	G1	G2	G3	G4	G5	G6	G7	G8	G9
Median	563	508	904	458	261	741	739	832	594
Mean	661,8	548,4	1028	605,6	347,8	872,9	718	889	735
Min.	241	322	591	153	87	537	149	564	246
Max.	1620	892	2433	2110	990	1851	1558	1326	1571
Std. Dev.	397,9	174,4	426,5	490,8	272,1	376,7	465	197	446

Table A-10: Descriptive statistics for outperformer participants over complete experiment (in seconds)

Task	J1	J2	J3	J4	J5	J6	J7	J8	J9
Median	382	308	535	489	139	536	139	565	108
Mean	375	463,2	612	572,4	212,8	569	167,9	573,4	121
Min.	124	193	320	104	74	323	78	293	44
Max.	914	1590	1163	1423	673	1127	563	825	244
Std. Dev.	212	375	239	406,6	159	205	109,3	143,3	60,9

Table A-11: Descriptive statistics for outperformer participants over complete experiment (in seconds)

	Median	Mean	Minimum	Maximum	Standard Derivation
Total Time	9663	10074	6462	13469	1920

Table A-12: Descriptive statistics for outperformer participants over complete experiment (in seconds)

It should be noted that the group of the outperformers consists of 5 participants that started with Java and 12 that started with Groovy; a fact that is a possible indication that the developers in the Groovy starter group consisted of generally better developers. Results of the tests for normal distribution are next.

	Kolmogorov-Smirnov[a]			Shapiro-Wilk		
	Statistics	df	Sig.	Statistics	df	Sig.
Task1 Diff	.124	17	.200*	.975	17	.894
Task2 Diff	.249	17	.006	.824	17	.004
Task3 Diff	.160	17	.200*	.940	17	.324
Task4 Diff	.108	17	.200*	.970	17	.810
Task5 Diff	.093	17	.200*	.985	17	.989
Task6 Diff	.272	17	.002	.885	17	.038
Task7 Diff	.210	17	.045	.894	17	.054
Task8 Diff	.113	17	.200*	.949	17	.448
Task9 Diff	.222	17	.025	.870	17	.022

a. Lilliefors Significance Correction
*. This is a lower bound of the true significance.

Table A-13: Tests for normal distribution on differences between groovy and java times for complete experiment outperformers

Test results allow use of t-test on tasks 1, 3, 4, 5, 7 and 8. The results of the t-test and Wilcoxon test are shown in the table.

	J1 - G1	J2 - G2	J3 - G3	J4 - G4	J5 - G5	J6 - G6	J7 - G7	J8 - G8	J9 - G9
t-test Sig. (2-tailed)	.007	-	.001	.858	.147	-	.000	.000	-
Exact Sig. (2-tailed)	.009	.159	.001	.854	.207	.002	.000	.000	.000
Dominating Ranks	Java	-	Java	-	-	Java	Java	Java	Java

Table A-14: Results of t-test and Wilcoxon test for outperformer students of whole experiment

Results are confirmed significantly different by both tests for tasks 1, 3, 6, 7, 8 and 9. In all cases of significance, it is in favor of Java. This could mean that no matter which language the better participants started with, they were generally quicker in the Java part (although a major part of the better participants were in the Groovy starters group). Results for tasks 4 and 5 are not significant and suggest that the time needed to fix the semantic errors is not impacted strongly by the language used.

A.2.5.2.   Underperformers

Now the data and analysis for the underperformer group:

Task	G1	G2	G3	G4	G5	G6	G7	G8	G9
Median	563	508	904	458	261	741	739	832	594
Mean	661,8	548,4	1028	605,6	347,8	872,9	718	889	735
Min.	241	322	591	153	87	537	149	564	246
Max.	1620	892	2433	2110	990	1851	1558	1326	1571
Std. Dev.	397,9	174,4	426,5	490,8	272,1	376,7	465	197	446

Table A-15: Descriptive statistics for underperformer participants over complete experiment (in seconds)

Task	J1	J2	J3	J4	J5	J6	J7	J8	J9
Median	382	308	535	489	139	536	139	565	108
Mean	375	463,2	612	572,4	212,8	569	167,9	573,4	121
Min.	124	193	320	104	74	323	78	293	44
Max.	914	1590	1163	1423	673	1127	563	825	244
Std. Dev.	212	375	239	406,6	159	205	109,3	143,3	60,9

Table A-16: Descriptive statistics for underperformer participants over complete experiment (in seconds)

	Median	Mean	Minimum	Maximum	Standard Derivation
Total Time	9663	10074	6462	13469	1920

Table A-17: Descriptive statistics for underperformer participants over complete experiment (in seconds)

The underperformer group is made of 5 participants that started with Groovy and 11 that started with Java.

	Kolmogorov-Smirnov[a]			Shapiro-Wilk		
	Statistics	df	Sig.	Statistics	df	Sig.
Task1 Diff	.175	16	.200*	.919	16	.165
Task2 Diff	.211	16	.055	.722	16	.000
Task3 Diff	.130	16	.200*	.959	16	.644
Task4 Diff	.220	16	.037	.888	16	.051
Task5 Diff	.147	16	.200*	.930	16	.241
Task6 Diff	.116	16	.200*	.942	16	.372
Task7 Diff	.139	16	.200*	.951	16	.510
Task8 Diff	.180	16	.176	.927	16	.217
Task9 Diff	.213	16	.050	.871	16	.028

a. Lilliefors Significance Correction
*. This is a lower bound of the true significance.

Table A-18: Tests for normal distribution on differences between groovy and java times for complete experiment underperformers

Data from the tests for normal distribution show a t-test qualification of tasks 1, 3, 4, 5, 6, 7 and 8.

	J1 - G1	J2 - G2	J3 - G3	J4 - G4	J5 - G5	J6 - G6	J7 - G7	J8 - G8	J9 - G9
t-test Sig. (2-tailed)	.075	-	.090	.032	.205	.661	.000	.001	-
Exact Sig. (2-tailed)	.130	.274	.130	.051	.093	.528	.000	.001	.000
Dominating Ranks	-	-	-	-	-	-	Java	Java	Java

Table A-19: Results of t-test and Wilcoxon test for underperformer students of whole experiment

Only the results of tasks 7, 8 and 9 can be considered significant and are all in favor of the Java part. When not considering the obvious results for tasks 7 and 9, it seems that for the underperforming participants, the difference between the two languages becomes apparent only for task 8, which had the most types to identify. Tasks 4 and 5 results do not differ significantly (even if the results are close to being significant). But these results could too be biased because the majority of the group was Java starters.

A.2.6. Demographic of participants and Questionnaire Results

A total of 36 participants took part in the experiment. Some information on them is summarized here. 33 of the 36 finished all tasks, the other three had to quit at some part in the experiment due to various reasons. 30 of all participants were students, a mixed group of undergraduates and postgraduates. 3 were research associates and 3 practitioners from the industry. Only one participant was female, all others were male. 2 practitioners started with Java, 1 one with Groovy. The three research associates all ended up starting with Groovy.

The results of the questionnaire were collected for further research and their evaluation is not part of this work. Nevertheless, the results of the questions concerning programming skills and experience are shown here. The questions were

- How do you rate your general programming skills on a scale of 1 (worst) to 5 (best)? [GP]
- How do you rate your Java programming skills on a scale of 1 (worst) to 5 (best)? [JP]
- How many years of programming experience do you have? [Y]
- What was your mark in the programming course at this/another university? [M]

Below are the results of this questionnaire for all participants coded by their respective numbers [#].

[#]	0	1	2	3	4	5	6	7	8	9	10	11	12	13	14	15	16	17
[GP]	4	3	4	3	3	4	4	4	4	3	3	3	4	5	4	5	3	1
[JP]	3	1	4	4	3	4	4	5	2	4	3	4	3	4	4	5	4	2
[Y]	16	5	6	12	8,5	9	5	5	6	3	7	3	10	15	10	10	4,5	3
[M]	2,7	1,3	1,3	3,3	1	2,3	2,3	1,7	1,7	3	2,7	3	1	1	2	1,3	2,3	2

[#]	18	19	20	21	22	23	24	25	26	27	28	29	30	31	32	33	34	35
[GP]	4	3	4	5	3	5	3	4	4	5	4	4	4	4	3	5	5	4
[JP]	3	3	4	5	3	5	4	4	4	5	2	4	4	3	3	5	4	4
[Y]	5	8	8	7	10	8	5	7	8	18	12	7	10	5	3	5	8	10
[M]	2	1,7	3,7	3	3,3	2,3	5	1	1,7	1		3	2	2	2	1	1,7	2

Table A-20: Questionnaire results for programming skill questions

A.3 An Example of a problematic Experiment Design and Analysis

While explaining the experiment's design, it was mentioned that there are a few common errors made during the design of experiments. This chapter provides an example by treating the current experiment's results as if it had been designed as an independent-measure experiment where each participant had to solve only either the Groovy or the Java part (in contrast to the actual repeated-measure design that was really used). The group that started with Groovy is therefore now considered the "Groovy only" and the Java starters are considered the "Java only" group. That means that no within-subject analysis can be done, making the results at least quite questionable and doubts are appropriate considering their possible neglect of many unsystematic variances like learning and practice effects. The results of this fictive experiment are still shown below so that they can be compared to the actual results of this experiment.

First, a look at the corresponding descriptive statistics should be taken:

Task	G1	G2	G3	G4	G5	G6	G7	G8	G9
Median	709	516	976	801	416	880	813	862	750
Mean	822	616	1074	1022	539	992	758	1004	788
Min.	241	345	611	337	92	537	149	564	246
Max.	2215	1273	2146	3062	2262	1894	1492	1838	1712
Std. Dev.	491	233	386	726	510	412	436	326	472

Table A-21: Descriptive statistics for Groovy group of independent design (in seconds)

	Median	Mean	Minimum	Maximum	Standard Derivation
Total Time	6698	7616	4555	10869	1987

Table A-22: Descriptive statistics for Groovy group of independent design (in seconds)

Both the Groovy as well as the Java group results display a large spread in their scores. It is interesting that all descriptive scores are actually smaller for the Groovy group. This could possibly lead to the wrong conclusion that the tasks might have been easier to solve using Groovy. But it is much more likely that by factor of chance a larger number of good developers ended up in the group starting with Groovy, which would make the experiment's results meaningless. Unsystematic variance cannot be calculated by means of statistics, as there is no within-subject comparison because of missing values for the second part.

Task	J1	J2	J3	J4	J5	J6	J7	J8	J9
Median	662	938	940	1703	678	918	263	777	145
Mean	762	1195	1070	1614	794	1106	303	838	168
Min.	375	315	574	312	177	582	102	566	98
Max.	1609	4285	1983	2910	2264	3240	900	1514	535
Std. Dev.	331	948	417	679	621	652	193	221	107

Table A-23: Descriptive statistics for Groovy group of independent design (in seconds)

	Median	Mean	Minimum	Maximum	Standard Derivation
Total Time	7328	7850	4608	14414	2516

Table A-24: Descriptive statistics for Groovy group of independent design (in seconds)

When looking at the different task types, tasks 7 and 9 seem to be generally solved faster using Java (which is not surprising considering that the stakes were compile error vs. runtime error), a fact that is supported by a much higher mean rank and rank sum in the Mann-Whitney table of ranks below. It is interesting that although task 9 has a larger branch size, the times do not differ too much from the task 7 times. For tasks 4 and 5 (semantic errors), the results are again in favor of the Groovy part (both from descriptive values as from ranks). For the type identification tasks 1, 2, 3, 6, and 8, the Java scores seem only to be better for task 1 (the smallest) and task 8 (the largest), for all other tasks there is no huge difference, the Groovy developers seem to even outperform the Java-developers in some of them (tasks 2 and 6). In both languages, the type identification tasks do not show a clear trend that more types to identify necessarily needs a longer time.

The tests for normally distribution (the results are omitted here to keep this part short), especially the Shapiro-Wilk-test, produce no result that would permit the use of parametric tests. Therefore, only the Mann-Whitney-U test and in addition, the Kolmogorov-Smirnov-Z test were used to examine the results. The following table only shows the interesting values, those being the exact significance results from both tests. The first row shows the results of the Mann-Whitney-U test and the second the results of the Kolmogorov-Smirnov-Z test.

	Task1	Task2	Task3	Task4	Task5	Task6	Task7	Task8	Task9
MW-U Exact Sig.(2-tailed)	.901	.009	.852	.015	.217	.709	.003	.034	.000
KS-Z Exact Sig.(2-tailed)	.640	.022	.954	.005	.148	.686	.003	.139	.000
Dominating Ranks	-	Groovy	-	Groovy	-	-	Java	Groovy	Java

Table A-25: Results of Mann-Whitney-U (MW-U) and Kolmogorov-Smirnov-Z (KS-Z) test for independent design

Both tests (with K-S-Z said to have more power for small samples) detect a significant difference ($p < 0.05$) in the times of tasks 2, 4, 7, 8 and 9. The relevant values are the exact significance results.

To summarize, what do all of the above results explain? For one, there seems a clear trend that tasks 7 and 9 are solved quicker using Java; a result that seems to have been pretty obvious from the beginning. But the data do not harden the hypothesis 2-1 that a larger branch size (distance) from bug to error leads to a longer time of finding the bug. Although no test was done on this, the descriptive data really point towards no significance. Consequently, no conclusion can be drawn here, similar to the real experiment results.

Also, the hypothesis 2-2 that semantic errors need similar time to fix in both languages holds for task 5 (no significant difference), but not for task 4, where the Groovy group actually outperforms the Java group. It cannot be said whether this might be because there were better developers in the group, or bad developers in the other. There is no way to tell exactly because too many factors might be at work. Therefore, this hypothesis would have to be rejected, similar as in the real experiment.

The type identification tasks do not differ significantly between the two groups except for task 2; and this difference is even in favor of the Groovy group. Therefore, hypothesis 1 would have to be rejected, too. This contradicts the results from the actual experiment, where a genuine positive effect of static type systems was discovered.

As a final statement, it should now be clear why data from a problematic experiment design do yield problematic results. Compared to the results from the actual experiment that detected a genuine effect for the main hypothesis, this type of design and analysis would have not detected it and even would have yielded contradicting results in favor of the Groovy group. The knowledge from the actual experiment tells us that this was probably because the majority of the Groovy group seemed to have been more experienced developers. Had only the here presented and discussed independent design been used, this knowledge would not be available.